D0125507

THE CHURCH IN OUR TOWN

A STUDY OF THE RELATIONSHIP BETWEEN THE CHURCH AND THE RURAL COMMUNITY

ROCKWELL C. SMITH

REVISED AND ENLARGED EDITION

ABINGDON PRESS NEW YORK NASHVILLE

THE CHURCH IN OUR TOWN

Copyright MCMLV by Pierce & Washabaugh
Copyright MCMXLV by Whitmore & Stone

All rights in this book are reserved.
No part of the book may be used or reproduced in
any manner whatsoever without written permission of
the publishers except brief quotations embodied in
critical articles or reviews. For information address
Abingdon Press, 810 Broadway, Nashville 2, Tennessee.

Library of Congress Catalog Card Number: 55-8612

SET UP, PRINTED, AND BOUND BY THE
PARTHENON PRESS, AT NASHVILLE,
TENNESSEE, UNITED STATES OF AMERICA

254.2
Sm 6c
C.1.

Abingdon - Cokesbury

1.50

1 Nov. 63

FOR

ETHEL C. and STEPHEN G. SMITH

CHRISTIAN PARENTS

19474

FOREWORD

THIS BOOK is about a little church standing on the hilltop or clustered with school, shops, and homes upon the prairie expanse stretching away to the western mountains. And it is about a little town and the farm homes lying about it and looking toward it for those services which a family cannot by itself secure. It is not about all the things done in either the church or the town; it could not be, for no one could put down on paper all the rich events which characterize their lives. It is rather about those interests which the church and the town have in common. It is a book about the church looking out away from collections and organizations and budgets and apportionments to its people in their working world; it is about the other groups in and about the town looking in toward the church and discovering the message and the standard it has for their common life.

This is a book for churchmen; it is written for the men who are concerned that the little church shall express in its life the will of God. These men, both clergy and laity, know that the religious life is an infinitely rich one. It involves and stems from a faith in God—not an unknown or distant God, but a God who has revealed and reveals himself to us in Jesus. It offers a real and vital help from God in our lives now: we are to ask and seek and knock, because our God purposes to reward those who seek him. It continues in daily fellowship with God: his concern for our lives is not incidental or occasional but central and perpetual. Just as his love for us is the constant of the religious life, so our love is to go out to him with an

7

answering constancy and singleness; we are to love the Lord with all our heart and mind and soul and strength. And this same love is to permeate all our relationships to our fellows, so that the command is not simply to love God but to love our neighbor as we do ourselves.

Churchmen know that the church is that fellowship which gives expression to these elements in religion. In the church group we learn the nature of Christian faith in God: through the church group at public worship we come into that fellowship with God by which his constant help may be appropriated; through the fellowship of the church our own daily experience of God is given stimulation and guidance; and through the auxiliaries of the church our love for men is expressed and made vital. Best of all, the church supplies us with a sympathetic group of fellows within which we can try the disciplines of Christian love before we carry them out into the hurly-burly of the workaday world.

Churchmen also know that their lives are markedly influenced by other groups in which they participate. They are Christians first, but they are also citizens, Rotarians, Grangers, United Mine Workers, school-board members, participants in the total group life of their immediate community. And in this plural relationship of loyalty to various groups they often find their lives made fundamentally inconsistent. The help of God and his law of love seem distant and unreal within some of these other groupings, so that the Christian is tempted to accept for the time being other help and another law. This book is concerned with this fact in our common experience and with the responsibility of the Christian fellowship, the church, in remedying this situation. It insists that the church has a responsibility not only to the individuals who are its members but to the community environment of which it is a part, that indeed it cannot do its best for the members until it takes a responsibility for the other groups in which they must participate, and for the life of its community as a whole.

This, then, is a book about the church as a group among

groups. The church is like other groups in the people who make it up, the forces which continue its growth or hasten its decline, the conflicts which disrupt it, the leadership which directs it. It differs from them in that its reference is always to God. When it is true to itself, the church group asks in every situation not, "What is expedient?" or, "What do we want to do?" but, "What does God want us to do?" It is this unique loyalty to an authority beyond its immediate membership which at once distinguishes the church from other groups in the community and makes it a source of help and strength to them.

I have attempted to bring together in these pages materials from the academic disciplines of rural sociology and agricultural economics as they bear upon the work of the rural church. While the book is written with the churchman particularly in mind, the social scientist may discover certain values in it. For one thing, he will see how his own studies are appropriated by a professional religious leader. I have served as a rural pastor in New England and the Middle West for twelve years. Here the social scientist will get a preacher's view of rural sociology and agricultural economics. Perhaps his conclusions will seem to him to have been misunderstood and misapplied, in which case he ought to set me right. On the other hand, putting his conclusions to the test of action may serve to indicate to the scholar some of the areas in which he still needs to delve. Against the background of church life the unfinished business of social science becomes more clear.

In these pages, as in my life, I am particularly indebted to Dr. John H. Kolb and the late Dr. George S. Wehrwein, of the University of Wisconsin. They have taught me all I know technically of rural life. Standing in the great liberal tradition, they have never hidden from civic responsibility behind the scholar's gown but have rejoiced to play the part of men among men in the arena of life's pressing decisions. They have served the people of Wisconsin and the United States in a spirit which the church may be proud to recognize as its own.

This book was written in answer to a sermon preached by Dr. William K. Anderson, secretary of the General Conference Commission on Ministerial Training of The Methodist Church, at a pastors' school in North Carolina. Dr. Harris Franklin Rall, of Garrett Biblical Institute, and Dr. J. M. Ormond, of Duke University, read the manuscript and gave me the benefit of their criticisms. President Horace G. Smith of Garrett graciously allowed me the time I needed to work on the manuscript.

M. Leslie Infinger, my secretary, has been patient with my illegible pages and efficient in handling every detail of putting them into type. Most of all I stand indebted to Frances Eckardt Smith, my wife, who has stood by with red pencil in one hand and a pat of encouragement in the other to keep me going until the work was done. And we both stand indebted to the Christians of Belchertown, Ludlow, and Ware, Massachusetts; Belleville, Wisconsin; and Hinckley, Illinois; with whom we worshiped God in the countryside. With so many good helpers it can only be my fault if there are errors of fact or conclusion in this book.

ROCKWELL C. SMITH

FOREWORD TO THE REVISED AND ENLARGED EDITION

The passage of time, the accumulation of new data, and social change have made it necessary to revise this book. The acceptance my brother ministers have accorded my work has made such revision acceptable to the publishers. For that acceptance I am grateful. I hope these pages show how much I have gained from the criticisms of my readers.

My own resistance to recognizing the social-class system in rural America, an inadequate understanding of the relationship of farm prices to land tenure, and a somewhat less than humble attitude of criticism toward organizations and agencies with

10

whose policies I did not agree are among the faults in the first edition which I have tried to remedy in this. Humility in these matters is not simply a private virtue; it is prerequisite to that social knowledge and action on which the future of our culture depends.

To my students I stand in particular debt for stimulation and growth. Miss Gloria Laubheimer, my secretary, has typed this manuscript with efficiency and dispatch in the midst of an already overloaded schedule. I thank her and the many others whose sacrifice has made these pages possible.

R. C. S.

CONTENTS

13

1

WHAT DO WE MEAN BY "RURAL"?

IN A world of change words often stand still. "Give a dog an ill name," George Colman the elder said, "and hang it." Something of the stability and inflexibility of the word shapes our perceptions of the object so that, unless we continually check our words against experience, we end by living in an unreal world. Nowhere is this danger more apparent than in our use of the word "rural." The majority of Americans now live in cities, but they came originally from open country and small town. When phrases like "rural," "town and country," "old home town," are used, we import into them the sentimental memories of our youth. Or we may generalize our own peculiar sectional experiences as easterners or southerners or westerners and look at rural life everywhere as if it were like that rural life in which we once participated. Actually change and diversity characterize rural life in America, and knowledge that goes back as little in time as ten years is an unreliable guide to the paths of contemporary rural life.

United States Census definition

One of our stereotypes for the word "rural" is "farm." We know that there are a few businessmen and professional people out there, too, to serve farmers; but we picture the rural community as dominated by farmers numerically and psychologically. Any program for community betterment based on this identification misses the mark. Rural population not only includes a substantial proportion of persons who are not farmers, but between 1940 and 1950 the farm population became a minority in the total rural population. This happened in spite of the fact that 7,500,000 Americans were moved from the rural nonfarm to the urban category by a change in United States Census definitions. The new definition includes as urban all persons living in population units of 2,500 or more, whether incorporated or not, plus persons living in population units below the 2,500 level which are contiguous to cities of 50,000 or more. All other persons are classified as rural, with those living on farms called "rural farm" and all other persons called "rural nonfarm." Of our 150,500,000 Americans in 1950, 96,-500,000 were urban in this new sense, 23,000,000 were rural farm, and 31,000,000 were rural nonfarm. Less than one in six Americans was a farm resident, and the farmers were outnumbered in the rural population itself four to three. Table I below gives the detailed figures.

TABLE I
United States Population, 1950

CLASSIFICATION	NUMBER	PER CENT
Urban	96,467,686	64.0
Rural Farm	23,048,350	15.3
Rural Nonfarm	31,181,325	20.7
TOTAL	150,697,361	100.0

There are additional numerical division points. The census itself used 8,000 and 4,000 before arriving at the 2,500 figure in 1910. The Division of Home Missions in the National Council of Churches of Christ in the United States of America sets 10,000 as the dividing line, reserving work in communities of less than 10,000 to its Department of Town and Country Church. In this it is followed by the home or national mission boards of the denominations. When the phrase "town and country" is used, it has this statistical meaning. In general a treatment of rural community problems and their opportunity for the church must depend upon the United States Census definition, however, since most of our statistics are given to us in its terms.

One who has experienced the vital tides of rural life is bound to feel restless and unsatisfied by any merely numerical discrimination. Statistics are important; we dare not neglect them in the interest of the definite and reliable light they throw on our problems and our performance in solving them. Nevertheless we need always to press beyond the merely statistical even though efforts at definition in the area of meanings must be less clear and definite. Can we find qualities at the center of societies, urban and rural, in which these societies differ as ways of life? If we can, if these societies have differing styles which we can describe, then we shall have powerful tools for understanding the dilemmas and conflicts our present society faces and for integrating the church and its program in its community setting.

A comparison of rural and urban types

Science has progressed directly as it has been able to abstract from the whirl of events and experience certain concepts in terms of which the whirl takes on meaning and order. Such a concept is that of the perfect plane, the absolutely flat surface. Nowhere in even as highly a developed technology as our own is there a perfectly flat surface. All surfaces subject to the scrutiny of a microscope resolve into mountains and valleys. Nevertheless, the conception of a perfectly flat surface has given the physicist power to deal with the approximately flat surfaces of our real world. A fictional idea gives power over actual reality.

Similarly social science deals with fictional abstractions which cast suggestive light upon actual social conditions. In such a fashion we define and distinguish urban and rural societies. We set up two types of society poles apart, representing extreme contrasts. In doing so we agree that neither extreme is found or ever has been found on this earth. They represent rather the synthesis of the significant tendencies which we find at work in actual urban and rural societies. Between the extremes which we picture exists a continuum along which existing societies may be ranked in terms of their relative urbanity or rurality. Thus our types become bench marks against which actual societies may be judged and in terms of which they may be compared. By the device of these exaggerated descriptions we hope to make clear what most characterizes urban and rural life wherever and in whatever degree each is found.

Social unit

Our procedure here will be to compare these types of society on seven traits or characteristics. The first such characteristic is the basic social unit of each society. For rural people the basic social unit is the family. Work, play, prayer, are all family matters. Reputation and position with other persons in the neighborhood or community are predicated upon the standing of the family. I am not known first of all for myself in rural society; I am known first of all as "Steve Smith's boy." Resources, possessions, abilities, are first familial and then my own. Life itself is lived almost completely within or in terms of the family circle. The family is looked upon to supply not only space and resources for living together but also the values, the activities, and the rewards which make living at all significant.

By contrast, the social unit of urban life is the individual. Work is an individual matter. Indeed, the worker's working space is almost always geographically separated from his living space. Play and religious activity are likewise separated and departmentalized. The family is chiefly a consumption unit in the city. Social status is not accorded or denied in terms of the individual's familial setting but rather in terms of his own personal gifts and graces. In the city men are counted one by one.

Social contacts

A second contrast has to do with the social contacts characterizing each type of life. In urban society social contacts are categorical; that is, we meet and know other persons in terms of the specific functions they perform in society, not as whole persons or in the light of the totality of their experience and character. We may even know a person quite well in daily contacts and be on some degree of intimacy with him without knowing more than the little segment of his personality which is affected by our common business. We may visit the city post office frequently and receive as well as give courteous consideration in our interaction with the post-office clerk. We may get to the point of exchanging pleasantries and having our own private jokes. Yet all we know of the man is that he is a clerk at the window in such and such a post office. We do not know that his wife has diabetes, that his daughter works for the telephone company, that his son is finishing a graduate degree in law at the University, that he is a Disciple of Christ, and that he is an enthusiastic fly fisherman. The most significant and certainly the most interesting qualities of the man are lost in the post-office clerk.

Contacts in rural society are sympathetic and personal; that is, they involve knowing a person, not in a single function of his life or along a tiny segment of his personality, but in all his activities and relationships. Among rural persons a man is first of all himself in his totality and then a functionary in his specific task. A visit to a rural post office is a far different thing from the visit to an urban institution described above. To ask the postmaster for one's mail is almost discourteous. We begin a conversation with him which may, and probably will, include the weather, the crops, our physical health and that of our wives, the fate of various candidates in the coming election, and the price of milk on the Chicago milkshed. Only after we have revealed the full range of our personalities to each other does he reach somewhat apologetically toward our box and bring out a handful of mail. "John writes that he's coming home this week end," he explains, reviewing the few lines on the card, "and here's the new Sears-Roebuck catalogue."

Social bond

Rural people are united socially by the bond of custom. Their relationships are predicated, not upon formal agreement or legal enactment, but upon those unwritten laws which have been the evolution of centuries of human practice. Among rural persons a man's word is stronger than any bond he might give; indeed, rural persons are suspicious of anyone who prefers a bond more formal than that of custom. Actions are entered upon and relationships are sustained, though they may prove to be burdensome and expensive, because unwritten standards define such actions and relationships as essential to an honorable life. At the young adults' social the bank cashier hands a sheaf of bills to a farmer friend who has been too busy in the fields to get into town during banking hours. Almost as an afterthought, he remarks: "Drop in to sign the note when you're in town again."

Urban people are united socially by the bond of contract. A man's word is not enough; you must have his "name on the dotted line." Rentals are by written lease; laborer and employer are related by a written contract; automobiles, furniture, clothing, are sold through formal sales agreements. A man is primarily concerned, not with delivering a superior product to consumers, but with delivering goods which, however inferior in certain respects, will fulfill the letter of his contract. This does not mean that urban people are dishonest, but rather that their standards of honesty and dishonesty are determined by a literalism and a legalism based upon contractual considerations.

Social values

The social value of rural people is tradition. They prefer "old tried and true." The established, the fixed, the ancient, define the social arrangements which they prefer and support. A Methodist district superintendent, bent on rationally realigning two overlapping country circuits to make an obvious saving of transportation and time in their service, presented this plan to the two quarterly conferences involved. To his amazement, the suggestion was unanimously rejected by both conferences, the only argument offered against it being, "We never did it that way before." Tradition is the social value of rural people.

Over against this, urban people value novelty. Not the old but the new is their passion. A hat is judged, not by its conformity to the head of the wearer or its aesthetic excellence, but by its conformity to the most recent style. It is the fashion or fad that must be fitted in the city. And this overvaluation of novelty spreads to every field of life. It is at the root of the restlessness of city people. Here new gospels have their hearing, cults flourish, occult philosophies have their disciples, and political panaceas are accepted and pressed only to be discarded as they become something less than the latest news from tomorrow's utopia. Luke, in describing the Athenians to whom Paul addressed himself on Mars Hill, records: "For all the Athenians and strangers which were there spent their time in nothing else, but either to tell, or to hear some new thing."

Social control

Every society must develop means of social control when the fabric of family or neighborhood or community life is torn. Rural people turn to direct action to meet the emergencies which confront them. A neighbor breaks his leg just at the beginning of the planting season. Next Sunday at the little neighborhood church the pastor is asked to read the following announcement: "The neighbors will meet at the Jim Pence place on Tuesday of this week to put in Jim's corn crop. Come by eight in the morning and bring your tractor and tools." And eight o'clock on the morning in question will see several tractors lined up ready to enter Jim's fields, prepare the soil, and drill the corn in a single day. Furthermore, all summer long the neighbors will tend Jim's corn, if that is necessary because of his illness. Family emergencies and dislocations are met by direct action.

Even major social cataclysms are met in this pattern of direct action. In the great depression Iowa farmers devised the penny sale as a means of keeping banks and insurance companies from foreclosing on farm properties. On the day of a sale, the neighbors would gather at the farm in question and begin to bid in the property, fixtures, stock, and tools at a few cents per item. If a bidder for the selling agent appeared ready to interfere, he was quietly surrounded by farmers armed with pitchforks. Under such circumstances it was necessary only for the farmers to stand quietly with their pitchforks in hand to secure a sale without any outside interference. Feuds and lynchings are even more extreme illustrations of rural direct action, which clearly may become not only dangerous, but morally indefensible.

In the city, by way of contrast, social control is delegated to the agency. Cities abound in agencies for the prevention of cruelty to animals or to children; for the maintenance of family welfare; for the prevention and treatment of tuberculosis, cancer, syphilis. And this departmentalization of need, with its consequent division of the personality or the family, ultimately requires a co-ordinating agency to unify and bring together the personality or the family originally torn apart by the agency system. Violence in urban life is almost always an indication of personal or social breakdown, not an effort to remedy such breakdown.

Social environment

Most people are conscious of the contrast in environment of urban and rural people. The intimate and conditioning environment of the urban person is modern mechanical technology. He lives amid technologies and the products of technologies which free him from many of the uncertainties and discomforts of an unprotected life. Distance, the weather, drought, and heat have little meaning for him. Those natural uncertainties of which the farmer is so conscious are relatively unknown in any significant sense to the urban dweller. Coal for him comes in a truck from the dealer; he is almost entirely unconscious of the danger and drama attendant upon its production. For him law is largely a matter of convention. Church-school teachers report that it is all but impossible to teach city children, whose experience scarcely ever brings them into contact with nature and its laws, that there exists such a thing as an objective moral law. Experience of rules as man-made and man-changed leads people to think of all rules as being of this kind.

Rural people are more familiar with nature than with technology. Church-school teachers have no need to argue with rural children about the objectivity of moral laws. Such children are conscious from their earliest years that we live in a world in which we cannot have our own way. Hail comes and destroys the wheat. The whole season's work is lost. Both father and son stand helpless before the onslaught of the elements. The green wheat withers to the ground unless the rains come. Human convention or agreement cannot alter this. All that man can do is to know nature in its inexorable laws and then co-operate with those laws for the harvest. The significant environment for rural people is nature.

Social focus

There is finally the question of the social focus around which groups form in each society. Among rural people the focuses around which significant groups are formed are kinship and locality. The two key words in the social life of rural men and women are "kin" and "neighbor." Here "kin" has a much broader interpretation than in the city. It refers not merely to the immediate family but to a wide circle of in-laws and collateral descendants. And to each of these members of the wider family circle a kinsman's responsibilities are owed. Neighbor means, for rural people, the man next door. Grim experience has taught countrymen that the man on the other side of the line fence is very much their business. Russian thistles allowed to grow on one farm spread to the other farms around it. A gully caused by careless tillage on a side hill does not respect the line fence as it cuts back. Fences down on one farm mean crops ruined by the cattle on another. Kinship and geographic proximity are the focuses of rural group formation.

In the city, relationships of interest take precedence over blood and neighborhood relationships in the growth of groups. City men and women enter into social relationships with others who have the same interests as they, regardless of kinship or dwelling place. The next-door neighbor of the apartment-house dweller may be a man whose name he knows only as he reads it on the mailbox in their common hall. As for kinship, outside the immediate family it has little meaning. Urban families are sundered from relatives so often, and their mobility is so high, that relationships based upon kinship become attenuated and lose any significant power. The force which unites men and women in groups in the city is identity of interest. Persons concerned about the same matter come together and associate themselves in terms of this specific concern. Outside their common concern and its group expression they have little to do with one another.

Summary

I have sketched two contrasting patterns of life—two extremes between which actual rural and urban societies may be arrayed. I repeat that the pictures I have drawn have been purposely exaggerated to bring out significant points of difference. Nowhere does there exist a rural society exactly like the one described. And actual rural societies are in constant movement along the continuum at one point of comparison or another. In the last ten years, for example, American agriculture has moved rapidly toward the urban pole in its appropriation of the fruits of our machine technology. What we do observe empirically is societies tending toward approximately the sort of pattern I have drawn. This pattern is in process of change as urbanization affects rural society and as rural society contrariwise affects urban. But regardless of change there are always two ways of life more or less resembling the contrasting ways we have described. The variations are graphically pictured below:

ITEM OF COMPARISON	RURAL SOCIETY	URBAN SOCIETY
1. Social unit	Family	Individual
2. Social contacts	Sympathetic	Categorical
3. Social bond	Custom	Contract
4. Social values	Tradition	Novelty
5. Social control	Direct action	Agencies
6. Social environment	Nature	Technology
7. Social focus	Kinship and locality	Common interest

Other contrasts are sometimes added, and a word ought to be said about one in particular. People often insist that rural persons are isolated, whereas urban persons are not. Such a conclusion is inaccurate and undiscriminating. Rural persons are often isolated geographically. At best they live in small clusters, with other neighbors and large centers of population remotely related to their lives. But city people are isolated too—socially isolated. Thrust by the intense interdependence of city life into constant and continual contact with other persons, they enter into only the most peripheral and transitory relationships with most of those with whom they are thrown. No one could be more thoroughly left alone and lonely than the ordinary inhabitant of a large hotel in the city or the casual traveler on an "el" or subway train. It is not that the rural person is isolated and the city person is not; it is rather that each has his own particular type of isolation.

In this book the term "rural" will refer to people whose lives are shaped by and reflect a culture more nearly like that I have described as rural. The traits we have discussed condition the atmosphere—personal and social—within which the rural church lives and in which the pastor of that church must build and conduct his program. Throughout our discussion we shall constantly return to this comparison to ask whether or not a specific activity or program is devised to meet the needs of rural people. And I shall insist that the work of the church is to safeguard and conserve what is essentially rich in this way of life, while it amends and redeems whatever is evil.

2

THE FRAMEWORK OF RURAL SOCIETY

THE RURAL persons with whom we have been dealing in the preceding chapter are not so many integers or atoms unrelated or casually related to one another. If we could look down upon the United States from somewhere in the stratosphere, we would note that rural persons live and behave in clusters and that these clusters are related to the space people occupy. We would note that they are clustered first of all in families, nonfarm families living in clusters of other nonfarm families, farm families living for the most part in relative spatial isolation from other families. To Americans this seems a natural relationship; if you ask an American group the question: "Where does a farmer live?" you will almost always receive the answer: "On a farm, of course." But the majority of the world's farmers do not live on their farms at all. They live in villages and go out to the field they till each day. Generally this is true in Britain and on the Continent, though Welsh farmers often and Norwegian farmers on occasion live on their farmsteads. Village-centered living for farmers is the characteristic pattern for such agricultural giants in the Orient as India and China.

American Land Settlement

To understand the pattern of on-the-farm settlement which characterizes so much of the United States, we must remember our historical background. The western frontier beyond the mountains from the colonial seaboard was settled by pioneers who poured over the mountains in advance of the Congressional Survey which laid out the Federal Lands and opened them for settlement. On occasion a pioneer would find a convenient acreage, clear his land, and build his log cabin, only to discover that the land he occupied had been sold by the government to an eastern speculator. This practice of selling land that one man had improved to another seemed entirely unjust to the frontiersman, and he reacted against it by developing the concept of "squatter sovereignty." This meant that the first man to settle on land and to improve it should have the first right to purchase it when it was put up for sale. A constant pressure from the frontier impinged upon the Federal government to make the principle of squatter sovereignty the formal law of the land. Finally Congress in the Preemption Acts established as procedure that, if a man had settled on a parcel of land, had built a house thereon, and had brought the land into cultivation, he should have an opportunity to submit the first bid for that parcel of land when it was put on sale. Further it was provided that, if he bid the minimum price for the land, no one was permitted to bid against him. This made squatter sovereignty into legal principle. When the Homestead Act was passed in Lincoln's first administration, it carried the procedure of settling on land into the machinery of securing free land. A settler was given 160 acres of land for the filing fees if he could prove that he had built a house upon it and brought the land into cultivation while living on it over a period of five years.

The Congressional Survey laid out the western lands in townships, areas of land six miles square. Each such township could be located and identified by its relationship to a base line which established its north-south position and a principal meridian which established its east-west position. Historically there have been seventeen principal meridians set in the continental United States and associated with each a base line. A township's position is given thus: Township Six South, Range Two West of the Third Principal Meridian. Such a township would be the sixth township measured south from the base line in the second tier of townships west of the meridian involved. Within each township are thirty-six mile squares, each one called a section of land. These sections are numbered from the northeast corner across and down shuttlewise to the southeast, as in Figure 1. In Canada the same system is used, but the numbering of sections is from the southeast corner. One of these mile-square sections includes 640 acres of land. Sections are divided into quarters called quarter sections, each of which contains 160 acres of land. Thus the unit of land to be homesteaded under the Homestead Act was a quarter section. Quarter sections within a section are designated northeast, northwest, southeast, and southwest. Thus a farm may be located within the United States without reference to such political boundaries as counties or states. Valley Farm, the boyhood home of President-Emeritus Horace G. Smith of Garrett Biblical Institute, is thus described: the Southwest Quarter Section of Section 6, Township 31 North, Range 5 East of the Third Principal Meridian.

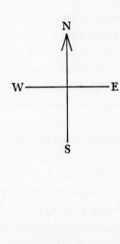

6	5	4	3	2	1
7	8	9	10	11	12
18	17	16	15	14	13
19	20	21	22	23	24
30	29	28·	27	26	25
31	32	33	34	35	36

A Survey Township. Its dimensions are 6 miles on each side; it contains 36 mile squares, each called a section, numbered from the northeast corner. Section 13 is divided into quarter sections.

When we combine the requirements of the Homestead Act with the facts of the Congressional Survey, we see at once that spatially isolated settlement was the pattern determined for the majority of American farmers. If a man must live on his land to get it, then no man can have more than three close neighbors and be a farmer. Four friends can settle in a little cluster on the near corners of their adjoining quarter sections; but then the nearest point of settlement must be at least half a mile away where another homesteader can settle on his land. The American Congress did not intend to establish a pattern of scattered settlement for American farmers, but the provisions of the Preemption and Homestead Acts did fix such a pattern. With this background we are in somewhat better position to understand the spatial pattern of American rural life.

The family unit: in the midst of its work

The first unit of rural society is the family. I have already pointed out with emphasis that rural people are family centered. And the rural family, because it is a real unit, has certain characteristics which distinguish it from the family in urban life. For one thing, the rural family lives in close association with the occupation of the family head. Making a living and living itself are closely and immediately connected in a single vital unity. We are all familiar with the fact that the farmer lives with his family in the midst of his farm. The farm kitchen becomes in turn the repair shop for small machinery and tools, the nursery for ailing lambs in the spring, or the setting for family consultations on farm practice and procedure of a winter evening.

What is obviously true of the farm family is equally true of other rural families. The members of the miner's family live constantly under the shadow of his occupation. His work is a very real part of their life. Around the family supper table is decided the momentous question as to how he and the grown sons shall vote in the union election. Here the father and brothers air their grievances and begin their discussions of what actions their union shall take. Here are forged those bonds of understanding and fundamental sympathy which bring the whole family to the picket line.

So it is also in the textile mill village or in the ordinary small trading center. The family presents a common social front to its world; it works as a unit, consumes as a unit, plays as a unit, thinks as a unit, worships as a unit. Among rural people generally, family authority and family solidarity are high.

Many children

A second characteristic is that rural families are relatively large. We customarily measure relative fertility by a fertility ratio—that is, the number of children under five per thousand women fifteen through forty-four. Women in these ages include virtually all the potential mothers of a population. Children under five are the product which this potential is producing. To discover the fertility ratio of any particular population, we divide the total number of children under five by the total number of women in the ages fifteen through forty-four and multiply by 1,000. We use children under five, rather than children born, because the larger age coverage factors out unusual infant mortality and indicates something of the stable, viable product of any given population. In 1950 a fertility ratio of 339 was required to maintain a stable population. In that year for the entire urban population of the United States the fertility ratio was 435; for the rural nonfarm population it was 551; for the rural farm population it was 597. The corresponding figures for 1940 were 256, 399, 484. It is clear that there has been a marked increase in fertility of all categories in our population in the last decade, with the urban population now more than reproducing itself. It must be noted, however, that rural rates are still much higher than urban; this supports the contention that rural families, farm and nonfarm, are relatively large.

Limited contacts

A third characteristic is that rural families have fewer neighbors and fewer contacts outside the family circle than their city cousins. It is not unusual for a week to go by in which the farm wife sees only her immediate family and an occasional visitor from the nearby farmstead. The miner's family is limited in contact to those who live in the little mining village. The rest of the world is "across the mountain" as far as it is concerned. Such limitation of contacts makes for an increase of family self-sufficiency. Where family authority is administered fairly and with a democratic consideration for the rights of each member of the family, such intense interaction makes for happy and integrated family living and a deep appreciation of rural life. The farmer's son wants to take up the neighboring eighty; the miner's son is eager to enter the mine; the fisherman's boy yearns for the day when he may have a dory of his own. But where family authority is autocratic, the very intensity of interdependence makes for a long and smoldering sense of injustice, which often breaks out in either intrafamilial violence or a settled dislike of rural life and a fixed purpose to leave it far behind. From this point of view it is probably true that the best families and the worst families are in the country.

Seasonal employment

A fourth and final characteristic is that rural families are seasonally employed. Farmer, miner, fisherman—all have their seasons of intense activity followed by seasons of comparative quiet. Spring and summer on the farm are seasons when there is always something to do and something more that must be left undone. Fall and winter are times of comparative ease, when the undone things may be cared for and the family may enjoy an earned rest. This is dramatically true in wheat country, measurably less true in a dairy area; but everywhere rural people are accustomed to a rhythmic alternation between intense activity and relative rest.

A development of considerable interest is the marked reflection of this seasonality of agricultural and extractive employments in the industrial picture. In 1930 11.5 per cent of all farm operators reported that they had worked off their farms one hundred or more days during the preceding year. In 1950 23.5 per cent of all farm operators reported they had worked off their farms one hundred days or more in 1949. The man-power demands of high employment levels have attracted an increasing proportion not only of farm dwellers but also of farm operators into nonfarm employment for a substantial part of the year. This has new meaning for the seasonality of rural employment and incidentally the scheduling of programs and activities of rural institutions.

The rural neighborhood

Beyond the rural family lies the neighborhood—the second significant group in which rural persons participate, and the first outside the family. The neighborhood has been defined as that geographical area in which families neighbor. Ask a farmer to name the families with whom he visits, with whom he exchanges work, from whom he borrows tools, and to whom he looks in case of emergency. A limited list of names will appear, and most names will appear in all the functions we have listed. Others in the same locality will respond with much the same lists of names. Locate the farms on a map and connect with lines those from which persons interact in at least one of the above ways. Soon you will note a circumference on the map at which all the lines turn in and none, or a very few, move out. The boundary at which the majority of the lines turn in is the real boundary of a neighborhood.

Perhaps the families involved are conscious of their neighborhood and have a name for it. Here is the Turkey Hill neighborhood, its area largely determined by hills and woods which set it off from adjacent neighborhoods. Its members know where these boundaries are and are conscious of themselves as neighbors. Their children often come to church school together in a couple of cars, while the adults follow later for morning worship. In any affliction of one family the whole neighborhood suffers and helps. There is not a store or a church in the neighborhood. A small district school, to which only a few of the families send their children, is the only social agency of any kind. Yet the feeling of the vitality of the relationship existing among these familes is so strong that when one of the renters is forced to move by a change of property ownership, the wife weeps because she has to leave Turkey Hill.

The chief cohesive force in the neighborhood has been Ed Gay and his trucking service. For over sixty years father and son and now grandson have maintained for this neighborhood area a transportation service for farm products to a nearby city and a return haul of consumer goods. Originally the trip was by wagon or sledge and team, but a motor truck now does the actual work. Twice or three times a week Ed drove by each home and stopped, if hailed, to carry truck into the city or to place orders and secure merchandise for the housewife. He was ready to buy anything that the family wanted; reports even circulated that he had been seen in the women's department of a large city store judiciously measuring corsets for one of his neighbors with a carpenter's rule. His visits were as much social as business in their nature, and his business enterprise served as a rallying point for neighborhood solidarity. Through him news of misfortune in any one family went to all the families of the neighborhood. Through him concrete and practical messages of help were sent to persons in trouble.

On the other hand, a neighborhood may exist where there is little in the way of consciousness of its existence on the part of neighbors. There may be no name for the neighborhood and no agencies of common action. Persons when queried may indicate that there is no namable neighborhood; yet when questioned as to specific acts of neighboring, they quickly reveal that a real area of sharing and concern exists.

Open-country or hamlet churches are often the institutions of a neighborhood, and their vitality and the refusal of members to close what may seem from the outside to be an inefficient church are due to the fact that its members sense it as the servant of an ongoing social enterprise. Such churches often have only a few families of the neighborhood as formal members of the church, but auxiliary organizations, such as a women's group, will be found to have within their membership virtually every eligible person within the neighborhood limits. Beyond the family and supporting the family is the neighborhood. But recent studies by Slocum and Case raise the question as to whether the neighborhood has not ceased to exist at all in areas of rural America where population mobility is high.

The town-country community

Beyond the neighborhood lies the community. The concept of the town-country community is not a legal or political one. It stems from the pioneer work of Dr. Charles J. Galpin at the University of Wisconsin. Dr. Galpin was engaged by the university to make certain rural life studies in Walworth County, a rich agricultural county just north of the Illinois border. He bicycled along the roads of the county interviewing farmers. Earlier, in a study of Belleville, New York, he had been impressed by the way cultural, economic, social, and spiritual interests of farmers centered in a small village. As he cycled through the Wisconsin country-side, he noted the fact that the ruts leading from any farm lane into the highroad were never worn equally in both directions. Always a definite trend in either one direction or the other was discernible. Dr. Galpin came to the conclusion that if he could mark the place on the highway where lanes stopped turning south and began turning north, he would have determined one of the points in the boundary of a natural social area or community. Thus by driving out along the roads from a village he could mark that area of farmland which was tributary to and participant in the life of that particular village center.

A technique was speedily developed whereby such a community area might be determined through questioning the merchants, schoolmen, and churchmen at the center as to the participants in their services. By charting the limit of their service areas thus arrived at on a map, the community area was delineated. We shall discuss this technique at length in the next chapter and point out its applicability to the work of the church. Here I wish simply to point out the method by which Dr. Galpin, with the aid of other students in the field, empirically discovered the existence of an area of common interest and action about a small village. Students of rural society have come to define the community as persons and their institutions and agencies within an area polarized about a village center at which the majority of the persons secure the majority of their services—economic, educational, social, and religious.

Community lines do not follow township or county lines, except on rare occasions. A village located near the boundary of a county may serve persons living in two or even three counties. This discrepancy between legal limits and social forces presents one of the continual causes of difficulty and friction in rural life. The separate incorporation of the village center of the community raises an artificial barrier between townsman and countryman. Persons living south of the county line may be quite unable to vote for the officials of the village with which their welfare is most immediately related. School-district limits may arbitrarily divide and send to different schools boys and girls whose social life is essentially one. We shall find ourselves returning to this problem in its many ramifications again and again.

Students have found difficulty in determining in particular cases whether a small hamlet was a community center or merely a large neighborhood. Recent research by Frank Alexander and his associates in several state experiment stations has developed a manner of rating all locality groups as to their neighborhood and community characteristics. Locality groups are rated in terms of the actual services they offer to the population; they are also rated in terms of group identification. The ratings vary on services from "no services" through four intermediate categories to centers providing one hundred or more services; and on group identification from "no identification" through two intermediate categories to high identification, which describes groups in which individuals are known in the totality of their personalities and in which there are widespread and deep feelings of interdependence, sympathy, sentiment, and mutuality. This device enables us to determine whether a particular village or hamlet is assuming more of a community role or whether it is moving toward the neighborhood function.

Out into the world

It is through the community center that urban and rural life are linked in our day. Each village center is tributary to some metropolitan subregion dominated by a great commercial or industrial city. And these metropolitan subregions again do not follow state, or even in some cases national, lines, but link wide areas of territory under various political governments. The state of Wisconsin, for instance, is dominated by Chicago, Milwaukee, and Minneapolis-St. Paul. Only one of these cities lies within the state. A girl in northwestern Wisconsin told me that she was going to "the university" one summer. Since I was then in attendance at the University of Wisconsin, I at once began to compare notes with her as to courses. When it became clear that we were talking about two different situations, a question brought out the fact that she meant the University of Minnesota in the Twin Cities. Here was a girl born and reared in Wisconsin, teaching in Wisconsin, who when she spoke of "the university" meant Minnesota, because she was living within the Twin Cities subregion.

Beyond and above the metropolitan subregion is the region or section, such as the Old South or the Northwest. And beyond the region lies the nation, and the nation within its world setting. Any churchman in the rural community in our day needs always to be conscious of this totality of relationship. The rural community does not live of and by itself. It rests upon family and neighborhood; it reaches on to metropolitan subregion, region, nation, and world. It is important that we know the anatomy of the rural community; but such a knowledge, however refined and exact, can be only dangerous unless we go beyond the community to these wider circles of fellowship. In our day the warm flame of rural localism must be delivered from the smoke of provincialism if light is to be cast upon the pressing problems which are our common lot.

3

FITTING THE CHURCH TO ITS COMMUNITY

How CAN the working pastor discover the limits of the community within which his people live? That is the practical question. If, as has been pointed out, this vital social living space is not limited by legal or political boundaries, how are we to determine its extent and influence? Professional students of rural society have developed elaborate techniques for the discovery and charting of such areas of social interaction. Here we shall outline a relatively simple method for charting the areas of social interaction of a given group of people.

First, a good map

First of all, the pastor must have an adequate map of the area in which his people live. It should be a map sufficiently large to permit the noting of individual families: two miles to an inch is a good scale for the map of a farming area. A village map must, of course, have an even larger scale. Suitable maps may be secured in a variety of places. A trip to the county seat should be your first effort. Introduce yourself to the county agent and ask his assistance in securing just the map you want; or visit the county clerk, the county road supervisor, or the county surveyor. From one or another of these sources you should be able to secure satisfaction.

Incidentally, the pastor ought to take this first contact with the county agent (farm adviser) and other county officials as an opportunity for the development of personal friendships. Rural life, we have already noted, is characterized by personal and sympathetic contacts. This fact the pastor needs to keep in mind, particularly in the early days of his ministry in a new community. His eagerness to gather equipment and to get his program under way may lead him to an unintentional brusqueness of manner. Such impersonality of approach may alienate those who might otherwise be his closest allies. Much community conflict may be traced to just this sort of untactful dealing of one community group leader with the leader of another group. The pastor must afford the time to make his visit with the county official a friendly and a personal one. There is, of course, every reason for not imposing on the time of a busy man, but this fact should not lead to treating him as a convenience rather than as a fellow human.

The Post Office Department has some excellent maps published for the use of postmen on rural routes and made available to the general public. Write to the Postmaster General in Washington and ask for a list of areas mapped for rural delivery service. If your area is mapped, you are particularly fortunate, for such a map will show all houses, schools, and churches clearly marked, and it will be moderately priced. Do not go to your local postmaster for this assistance, for he is not permitted to give out such information or to supply maps. In mountainous or hilly areas detailed relief maps are helpful and can be secured from the United States Coast and Geodetic Survey, Department of Commerce, Washington 25, D. C.

Should all these sources fail, a letter to your state bureau of roads or highway department should yield information as to first-class county maps in assorted sizes available through that office. Maps from this source have the advantage of being drawn to a single scale so that if your community or neighborhood areas overlap county lines, as they often do, you can secure maps of the counties involved, cutting out and pasting together such sections of them as give the area you want to explore.

If you are using maps of two or more counties and pasting them together, be sure to specify in writing to the highway department that you wish the maps to be of the same scale.

Drawing community boundaries

With a good map in hand the pastor may begin his survey by looking carefully at the total area for which he has a responsibility. If his is a village church and the village has a population of around five hundred or better, then he probably serves at the center of a community area. If his churches— almost certainly there will be more than one—are in the open country, he will need to study their proximity, in terms of distance to be traveled, to a small village or villages. He will be fortunate if he finds that his circuit falls within the normal trade area of a single village.

This preliminary scanning of the map prepares the way for a detailed exploration of the community area. The village pastor should go to several grocers in the village, the hardware-store proprietor, the banker, the garage owner, the farm-implement dealer, the high-school principal, and ask each one to indicate how far out from the village on the various roads his farthest customer lives. Different areas for each service will be found when these points are connected with pencil lines. After the pastor has drawn several such trade areas, he will be in a position to make an approximate delimitation of the community in terms of that area in which the majority of the persons secure the majority of their services at the village center. The accuracy of such a delimitation may be checked by stopping at several of the farm homes at the border of the area and asking where the families do their trading. A little study and checking in this way will lead to a dependable picture of the real area of community interaction around a village center.

The pastor who has only open-country churches should make his preliminary study in terms of the village nearest the largest number of his people. His situation, as we have already indicated, will be happy if he finds that all his churches lie within the trade area of a single village. If they do not, then he will have to study another village center to determine its area as well. When he discovers that his people and their churches lie within two or more community areas, he has already a significant clue to the difficulty of operating his circuit as a unit. People whose everyday life does not bring them together in common social enterprises can scarcely be expected to see the importance of working together in the religious program of a circuit. The discovery that churches on a circuit belong to different communities also goes far to explain why such churches do not have, through their pastor, a larger effect upon social affairs in their communities. A pastor simply cannot be as effective in social, political, educational, and cultural affairs in two communities as he can in one. Such circuits ought to be reorganized at as early a date as possible so that the churches fall together within a single community area. Our ideal should be that no pastor cross community boundaries in serving a circuit except in missionary territory or under emergency conditions as a temporary expedient. The malpractice of combining churches to form circuits on a basis of salary adequacy alone must cease if we are to have a socially effective, rather than a socially thwarted, rural ministry.

The community defined as that area in which the majority of the people secure the majority of their services at the village center sets the standard for the church. It is the area which the village church at the center and the open-country churches on the circuit have to evangelize. It represents their Christian opportunity and responsibility. Their duty is to see that every person within the community area has an opportunity to enter the Christian fellowship, to know in his own experience the risen Lord, to socialize his abilities and his talents on a universal level. People within the community area have this opportunity only through the churches which serve them. We represent their only chance to become completely and maturely human, to rise to their proper stature as children of God.

Mapping the church constituency

Once we have defined the community area, our next step is to measure the church constituency. The pastor may naturally raise the question here as to why constituency, rather than membership, is taken as a measurement. My own conclusion on the basis of experience is that studies in Protestant churches which utilize membership figures are totally misleading. Full membership is defined by Protestant churches in terms of the formal acceptance of membership vows when a child has reached an age at which such an acceptance may rationally be made. Membership among Roman Catholics is counted in terms of baptized children, each person once registered as a Catholic remaining a Catholic except under the most extreme conditions of apostasy. Thus what we have when we compare Catholic with Protestant membership figures, as in the United States Census of Religious Bodies, is comparison of a population count with a formal membership count. A comparison more truly representing the situation is obtained when we make our measurement for Protestant churches one of constituency.

For practical purposes constituency may be defined as including:

1. All active resident members of the particular local church
2. All persons not members of another local church who participate in church activities in any of the following ways:
   a. Attendance at church services
   b. Contributions to the financial support of the church
   c. Membership in auxiliary organizations of the church, such as the church school, youth group, women's group
   d. Calling upon the church regularly for pastoral service
3. All infant children of persons in any of the above categories

Such an accounting gives the total personnel which the church and pastor are serving and establishes most precisely the influence and outreach of the church.

Where a constituency roll for the church does not exist, one is easily constructed by calling together the membership committee of the church and the presidents or chairmen or superintendents of the various auxiliaries and departments, and asking each of these officials to bring the roll of his particular organization. The secretary of the membership committee then reads from the church membership list alphabetically, and the names thus obtained are noted down, together with the names of persons in families not on the membership roll of the church but engaged in the work of some of the constituent societies. The procedure just described has immediate usefulness in the work of strengthening Christian personality, offering to the participants a real vision of the opportunities of the local church, opportunities which they may not have sensed before. It points out services which auxiliaries may render of which they have not previously been aware. The resultant constituency list becomes a mailing list for the church and a calling list for the minister.

Participation in such a listing has pronounced spiritual overtones. In one church progress was effectually blocked by a woman extremely active in all the work of the church, very vocal in her protestations of loyalty and piety, and yet so ill adjusted a person that she made her own home a place of unhappiness and alienated others from every cause she sought to support. Among her activities in the church was teaching a teen-age girls' Sunday-school class. Under her leadership attendance had declined to a faithful four or five. She was invited to sit in on such a constituency listing as I have described. As the list grew longer and longer, as the name of teen-age girl after teen-age girl was added, this woman grew more and more silent and preoccupied. At the end of the evening's work, most uncharacteristically, she had nothing to say. Within a few days she telephoned the pastor and asked if she might have an interview. When she came to see him, it was to talk about her own failure. She put it thus: "The other evening I counted twenty-four girls who should be in my Sunday-school class.

Only four or five of them do participate at all regularly. Since that night I have been trying to understand why I reach so very few. Little by little I have been forced to the conclusion that the only possible reason for my failure lies in myself. Will you help me to find out and to remedy what is wrong in me?" Such an opportunity was what her pastor had been seeking in all his dealings with her. Out of this interview grew a series of others in which this woman was restored to happiness in her home and usefulness in her church and community. The procedure began when she was forced to give attention to the objective evidence of her own inner failure.

To continue with our project: when the constituency list is completed, the residence of constituents should be plotted on the same map on which the community area has been previously drawn. When this plotting is inspected, it should reveal that constituents cover the whole community area. If there are blank spots within the community area which the church does not reach, then we must ask ourselves why this is true. Perhaps we shall find that there is a large Mennonite colony in one section of the community from which we should not expect to draw members. But perhaps we shall find what I did in one parish I served, that within a mile and a half of the church were boys and girls who did not know what a church was and did not understand when I used the word "religion." What had happened was that people on poor land had been neglected by the church and had gradually drifted into a state of religious illiteracy and apathy. Such a sad condition, sad as much for the life of the church as for the lives of the people, can be discovered only by comparing constituency with community.

Measuring participation

Beyond constituency we must press to a third dimension of study, the participancy of the church. By participancy we mean the persons who regularly enter into some specific activity of the church. Attendance at the Sunday service of worship will prove one suggestive measure on which to determine participancy. Keep a regular record of attendants at church for a period of three months, and then chart these attendants on the map of the community and constituency to see whether people are attending church from all the community area. One church discovered, when it mapped participancy in terms of Sunday-morning worship and of church-school attendance, that farm families were attending church worship from all over the community area but that they were not attending the church school. The reason was plain when the fact became apparent. The church school was held at 9:30 in the morning, and the farmers were dairymen; they simply could not finish their chores and be in town at an early hour. When the church school was placed after the morning worship service, farm attendance quickly rose to expected levels. A study of participancy thus gives us a valuable clue to the effectiveness of our program.

A measure of our ministry

Finally, the minister will not himself be satisfied until he has measured alongside these other considerations his own pastoral service. This he can do by keeping a record of his pastoral calls over a two- or three-month period and then charting these calls on his map. Is he covering the entire community area, or is he staying pretty close to his home base? Only as he checks his own activities against his community responsibility can he be sure that he is serving his people in their total spread.

William G. Mather, Jr., reported in 1934 a study of church participation among high-school youth in Allegany County, New York, which yielded the significant figures shown in Table II on page 47. The column at the extreme right goes far toward explaining the trends of the other columns. Quite apparently it is only as we are willing to get back on the dirt roads in our calling that people on the dirt roads will feel that religion has a vital meaning for them.

TABLE II

Percentage of High-School Students Members of Church and Church Organizations, and Percentage of Homes Visited in Last Six Months by Pastor

RESIDENCE	CHURCH	MEMBERSHIP YOUNG PEOPLE'S SOCIETY	SUNDAY SCHOOL	VISITED BY PASTOR LAST SIX MONTHS
Village	80.9	39.5	60.4	65.5
Paved Road	67.0	21.3	43.6	42.5
Dirt Road	48.7	10.2	46.1	38.4

Thus far we have dealt with these various dimensions of comparison in terms of spatial distribution alone. But we should also compare community, constituency, participancy, and pastoral service in other terms. One such basis for comparison is age and sex distribution. Here our tool is the population pyramid. Such a pyramid is really nothing more or less than a double bar graph on a percentage basis. Data as to age and sex distribution in the community may be secured from the United States Census, Population Reports, Second Series—the report for your particular state. Determine from your map what population divisions most closely correspond to the actual community area, and then use the population figures for those divisions for your community figures. It is impossible to get actual figures for the community area short of a house-to-house canvass, but the approximation from the census data will give very good results.

When figures are secured, they may be entered in such a table as shown beneath Chart I on page 51; then the percentages may be calculated and charted on the graph form. It should be noted that the unit for charting the percentages from the table is not simply linear but is the square equal to one per cent. There are one hundred such squares within the line which bounds the whole pyramid, not one hundred squares for male and one hundred for female. Thus any marked disproportion of male and female in a specific population is revealed by an unbalanced pyramid. If above forty-five the intervals are for ten years instead of five, the vertical dimension is doubled and the horizontal dimension is accordingly cut in half to obtain the proper area. A little experimentation will make the pastor adept at this sort of graphic presentation.

The shape of a pyramid tells us at once a great deal about the population it represents. If one side outbulks the other, we are made aware that we have here a disproportion of one sex as over against the other. This, of course, makes immediate special demands upon the program of the church. If the base bar on the chart is not longer than any other, we can be sure that in this population the birth rate is decreasing. Any unusual bulge or recess in the pyramid poses a special problem for us. "Why does our population have this unusual characteristic?" we are forced to ask.

Once we have the population pyramid for our community, we turn to the construction of similar pyramids for our constituency, participancy, and pastoral service. It is easy with the help of two or three established members of the church to divide the constituency of the church into age categories, and to classify the participancy as well, using a single attendance by a particular individual as a unit in his particular age and sex cell. Constituency and participancy pyramids should conform to the community pyramid. If they do not, it means that the church is not serving all the age groups or sex groups in its community equally well.

The following three charts represent a study of the community, constituency, and participancy of the Methodist church at McLean, Illinois. The pastor, the Reverend Raymond M. Krutz, made this study in the late winter and early spring of 1954. Chart I is an age pyramid of Mount Hope Township, McLean County, Illinois, approximately the community area of McLean village. The data represents a special tabulation of the 1950 population count made by the United States Census at the request of Mr. Krutz. Chart I is not strictly comparable with the other charts, since the data they contain is four years later. Nevertheless it gives us a substantial picture of the population base from which the McLean church draws its members and to which it bears a Christian responsibility. Chart II is a population pyramid of the members, both full and probationary, of the McLean church. In Methodist polity baptized children are probationary members of the church, so that this is a population count of Methodist families similar to, though not identical with, the constituency count suggested earlier in this chapter. Chart III represents the attendance at the morning church worship service for the Sundays January 31 through March 14, 1954. The attendants were classified in terms of age and sex, and a single attendance on any Sunday was the unit of enumeration used. The average attendance for the seven Sundays was 86.5, but over 150 different persons attended church at least once over the period.

Even a casual inspection of the pyramids raises questions for a concerned Christian. We note first the basic regularity of the community figures in Chart I and the irregularity of both the other charts. It suggests that the church is making a haphazard and unsystematic appeal to the people who are its primary responsibility. There is an obvious disproportion between the sexes. A sex ratio—that is, the number of men in the population divided by the number of women and multiplied by 100—is a commonly used means of comparing population. The sex ratio of the data in Chart I is 95.1—that is, 95.1 men for every 100 women in the community population. For the church membership in Chart II the ratio is 86.4 men per 100 women, a figure substantially below that of the population from which the members are drawn. In Chart III we come to the really shocking data, for here the sex ratio is only 48.5 men per 100 women. Over a seven-week period less than half as many men as women attended church. This certainly is a matter of real concern to any congregation.

Another basis for comparing populations is the fertility ratio —the number of children under five divided by the number of women aged fifteen through forty-four, multiplied by 1,000. Since women fifteen through forty-four constitute the body of potential mothers in any population and children under five are their product, this ratio is a simple means of assessing the relative fertility of any particular group. In the community population of Chart I there are 513.4 children under five for every 1,000 women in the fifteen-through-forty-four category. In the church population of Chart II there are 447.1 children under five per 1,000 women fifteen through forty-four. This would indicate that church families are smaller than the families of the general population of the area. A fertility ratio is meaningless for the data of Chart III except as it indicates whether the families with children in the church population are bringing their children to church. The fertility ratio for Chart III data is 175.1, a figure only 34 per cent of that of the community fertility ratio and 39 per cent of that of the church itself. This would seem to indicate that young parents are not bringing their children to church. Does the church need to establish a nursery or develop some other technique for making little children and their parents welcome at divine worship? Is the low proportion of men in attendance due to the fact that many husbands are staying home with little children to allow their wives to attend church?

Finally we must be concerned that while 11.4 per cent of the community's population is sixty-five or older, only 6.2 per cent of Methodists, and only 6.9 per cent of attendants at the Methodist church, are in this older category. An immediate argument would excuse these figures on the ground that older persons are less able to participate in church activities because of their infirmities and poor health. The figures themselves will not permit this explanation, however, for people over sixty-five constitute one of the few categories in which church attendance is proportionately greater than church membership.

CHART I

AGE PYRAMID

PLACE

Mount Hope Township
McLean County, Illinois

DATE

U. S. Census, 1950
Special Count

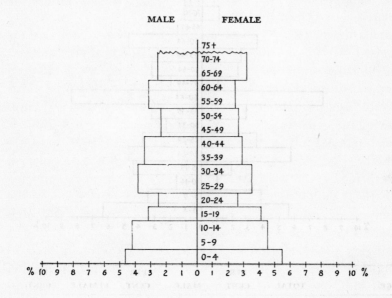

MALE   FEMALE

AGE	TOTAL	PER CENT	MALE	PER CENT	FEMALE	PER CENT
TOTAL	1,313	100.0	640	48.8	673	51.2
0-4	134	10.2	62	4.7	72	5.5
5-14	226	17.2	108	8.2	118	9.0
15-19	95	7.2	41	3.1	54	4.1
20-24	69	5.2	33	2.5	36	2.7
25-34	196	14.9	102	7.8	94	7.1
35-44	162	12.3	85	6.5	77	5.8
45-54	132	10.1	60	4.6	72	5.5
55-64	150	11.5	80	6.2	70	5.3
65 and above	149	11.4	69	5.2	80	6.2

CHART II

AGE PYRAMID

PLACE   DATE

McLean (Illinois) Methodist Church   March 15, 1954
Members and Probationers

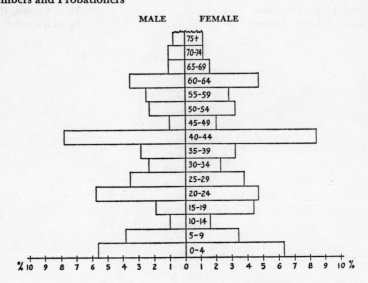

AGE	TOTAL	PER CENT	MALE	PER CENT	FEMALE	PER CENT
TOTAL	315	100.0	146	46.3	169	53.7
0-4	38	12.0	18	5.7	20	6.3
5-9	23	7.3	12	3.8	11	3.5
10-14	8	2.6	3	1.0	5	1.6
15-19	20	6.3	6	1.9	14	4.4
20-24	33	10.4	18	5.7	15	4.7
25-29	23	7.3	11	3.5	12	3.8
30-34	14	4.4	7	2.2	7	2.2
35-39	19	6.1	9	2.9	10	3.2
40-44	52	16.3	25	7.8	27	8.5
45-49	6	2.0	3	1.0	3	1.0
50-54	17	5.4	7	2.2	10	3.2
55-59	17	5.4	8	2.5	9	2.9
60-64	26	8.3	11	3.5	15	4.8
65-69	8	2.6	3	1.0	5	1.6
70-74	6	2.0	3	1.0	3	1.0
75-	5	1.6	2	0.6	3	1.0

CHART III

AGE PYRAMID

McLean (Illinois) Methodist Church
Attendance Morning Worship

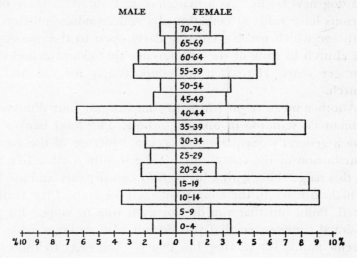

| | | PER | | PER | | PER |
AGE	TOTAL	CENT	MALE	CENT	FEMALE	CENT
TOTAL	606	100.0	198	32.7	408	67.3
0-4	31	5.1	9	1.5	22	3.6
5-9	26	4.2	13	2.1	13	2.1
10-14	76	12.6	21	3.5	55	9.1
15-19	58	9.6	7	1.2	51	8.4
20-24	29	4.7	13	2.1	16	2.6
25-29	10	1.7	10	1.7	0	0.0
30-34	29	4.8	12	2.0	17	2.8
35-39	67	11.1	17	2.8	50	8.3
40-44	82	13.5	39	6.4	43	7.1
45-49	27	4.4	8	1.3	19	3.1
50-54	28	4.6	6	1.0	22	3.6
55-59	47	7.9	17	2.8	30	5.1
60-64	54	8.9	15	2.5	39	6.4
65-69	23	3.8	5	0.8	18	3.0
70-74	19	3.1	6	1.0	13	2.1
75-	0	0.0	0	0.0	0	0.0

It seems clear rather that the church has not made any particular attempt to enlist the older citizens of the community, perhaps on the doubtful hypothesis that "you can't teach an old dog new tricks." As a matter of fact, many of these older persons have suffered bereavements and economic misfortunes with age which make them singularly open to the message of the church in spite of the indifference that characterized their younger years. Here is a real opportunity for the McLean church.

Another measure on which to compare our four dimensions is financial standing or annual income. The local banker can give a generally adequate and accurate picture of the income distribution of the community. Take to him a table like that on this page, along with a list of your constituents, and ask him to make a mark in the appropriate cell for each of the families listed. Point out that you do not want him to violate his professional confidences, that you do not wish to know what any specific family is receiving, but that you are eager to know how your people measure up in the light of total community. Ask in connection with farm families for "income for family living," not gross income.

Such a table in comparison with a general table for the whole community will give you a chance to determine whether you

INCOME LEVEL	NUMBER OF FAMILIES
Under $ 600	_____
$ 600- 999	_____
1,000-1,399	_____
1,400-1,799	_____
1,800-2,199	_____
2,200-2,599	_____
2,600-2,999	_____
3,000-3,399	_____
3,400-3,799	_____
3,800 and up	_____
TOTAL	_____

are reaching all groups in the community or not. Are we as churchmen neglecting to serve the very poor? There is some very significant evidence at this point.

In 1937 and 1938 William H. Sewell, of Oklahoma A. and M. College, made an exhaustive study of the social and economic status of eight hundred Oklahoma farm families. When he had the data on all these families for 123 different items, he divided them into four quarters, two hundred families in each quarter, according to relative standard of living. In the study he had secured data on church membership and church attendance of both husband and wife (attendance defined as being present at a minimum of one fourth of the regular services). What he found is revealed in Table III.

TABLE III

Church Membership and Attendance of Eight Hundred Oklahoma Farm Families by Standard-of-Living Quartiles

ITEM	RICHEST FAMILIES	UPPER INTER-MEDIATE	LOWER INTER-MEDIATE	POOREST FAMILIES
Husband Church Member	74.0%	53.0%	41.0%	23.5%
Husband Attends Church	77.9	65.3	54.5	40.5
Wife Church Member	88.0	72.4	57.5	33.0
Wife Attends Church	85.9	74.5	58.5	43.0

The most striking fact is that percentage of membership and participation regularly decline with a decline in the economic and social standard of the families. Over three fourths of the richest families regularly participate in church. Only two fifths of the poorest families regularly participate in church. Whatever the explanation, this a matter of deepest significance to the Christian church—a church for all people.

We have seen that people do not come to church one by one but that they come to church as members of significant groups all patterned together in the skein of a common community life. When the church acts in developing its programs without regard to this community life, it deals with its people in abstraction and not as they really are. Hence the importance of our knowing not only what we have in a community but also what the geographic borders of that community are. The methods we have outlined here give us a vital knowledge of the lines of social give and take along which the business, educational, and social lives of our people move. And this knowledge is a tool by which we can push the services of the church and the standards of religion out to the boundaries of the secular community.

4

LAND: TOO LITTLE OR TOO MUCH

ALL OF US live on the land. Urban and rural people alike depend daily for their basic livelihood upon the good earth. So efficient have our distribution systems been in the United States that many of us have forgotten our dependence upon the soil. It took the dislocation of distribution channels because of global war and the resultant rationing of scarce food products to remind us forcibly that we live on the land.

But why should the church be concerned with the land? After all, our business is relating people to God and to one another. Ought we not to leave matters of land and the use of land to the agriculturalist or the economist or the geographer and to concentrate upon the welfare of people upon the land? We can scarcely spend the time or secure the special knowledge and skill which would enable us to give professional advice as to land use. Is there not a danger that we shall try to do the work of the county agent or the soil-conservation expert and end by doing our people disservice?

Of course there is such danger—a danger which we must guard against here as elsewhere. We are to be experts in the relationships of man to God and man to man. But such relationships always involve relationships to God's creation—the land which we are instructed to inhabit. "The earth is the Lord's," and we are his stewards as we till the earth. It is not necessary that we become agricultural experts, but we must understand enough about agriculture to know the need for experts, to appreciate their programs, and to make their services available to our people. We are the connecting links between the everyday life of our people on the land and the experts who can bring to our problems their technical skill. Our business is not to answer questions and meet needs in this specialized field but to know what the questions are and to sense when the needs arise and to bring the resources available to bear upon the problems presented. Wherever land impinges upon the welfare of human beings, there the church and its pastor have a decided responsibility. Wherever land is treated in any way except as a gift from God, there the minister has a responsibility to declare such treatment a sin from which men should seek salvation and for which men must seek pardon.

When we speak of land, let us think in the most general terms, not exclusively of land under cultivation by the farmer, but of all the natural resources which God entrusts to our care. Land is soil, but it is also coal for fuel, oil for lubrication and power, ore from which metals and other chemical resources may be extracted. Land is all these things and more. Much of our discussion will deal with agricultural land, because it is there that many of our most acute problems lie in the United States; but what we say of it may be taken as an example of how Christian principles must be applied to all types and uses of land.

Too little room

The most obvious thing about land is that it is space. We are most conscious of this in connection with land in cities. There the location of a piece of land determines its value, and the use to which a piece of land is put is determined by where it lies. But space plays quite as important a part among rural people as it does in the city. In the city too little space is the problem; among rural people too much space poses an equal difficulty, for space must be traversed in getting goods to market, in securing the necessities of life for the home, in bringing children to school, in summoning a doctor for the sick, and in participating in the life of a church.

Before we discuss the problems incident to the abundance of space, we need to to realize that scarcity of space also affects rural persons under certain conditions. Too many people on a limited area of agricultural land may result in a situation of poverty and vice with which the church has a primary concern. China, India, and Japan are countries in which there is simply too little land to go around. For a vivid illustration of the problem turn to *The Japanese Village in Transition* by Arthur F. Raper and others, a study of thirteen villages in Japan carried out in 1947. The average farm studied consists of a little less than $2\frac{1}{2}$ acres of land lying outside the village in sixteen separate fields. Moreover, these fields do not all lie together but are scattered in different directions from the village. Such a limited land area leaves no surplus land for the grazing of stock. Only every third farm has a draft animal, and there is an average of one dairy cow to forty-two farms. There are few chickens, and, if a family has chickens, there are generally no more than four. Obviously the only way to survival under such circumstances is to apply all the labor possible to the meager supply of land in return for a bare existence.

Southern sharecroppers operating small acreages of cotton are in exactly the same position. Their incomes are very low because of the limited land they operate, and they have a long period of the year in which they have little or no employment. Among them poverty and leisure constantly tempt to cheap excitements and the grosser vices. And this is particularly evident in their religious lives. For the most part, because of their small farms, they do not have the economic resources to support an efficient church and ministry, while at the same time their isolation and leisure demand of religion an appeal to the grosser emotions which lends itself to an undisciplined expression. The indifference of organized religion to the poverty and religious need of these people has left them the dupes of ignorant or predatory and unprincipled leaders. We shall return in later chapters to a discussion of the plight of the sharecropper, but here it is important to point out that his difficulties arise in large part from the fact that he does not operate a large tract of land. The church has an interest in land as space.

Too much room

The other side of the problem is too much space. In many areas of the North and West much of our land is just so much waste space to get over. For the public it is so many miles over which roads, railways, and power and communications lines must be built in order to supply the needs of the people. There is no way we can do away with deserts, swamps, and wastelands; they stand as a constant drain upon our total public resources.

The chief burden of such excess space, however, falls upon the family that lives upon it or within it. Here is a farm family in northern Wisconsin living upon a relatively rich acreage of land in the midst of barren and largely infertile cutover lands left by the lumber barons. Within the generally light and sandy soils of northern Wisconsin are numerous pockets of rich and fertile earth. A family on such a farm can raise good crops even in the face of the long and bitter winter and the extremely short growing season. But what of harvesting, processing, and selling such crops? The thresher does not want to bring his machinery down the long, rutted road to their place. It may be damaged by the rough going, and there is little to be earned at the end of the road. It is hardly profitable to purchase a combine, for there are no neighbors to share its use. And when or if the crop is harvested, the price received for it is low because of the high charges for transporting the crop to a distant market. Such a farmer can operate successfully so long as he produces crops consumed upon the farm itself by family or stock. But he comes into the highly competitive market of the commercial farmer with the odds distinctly against him because of the large transportation charges which must be assessed against the prices received for the crop when marketed. If prices are high, he will make good, but any marked drop in prices will put him in the position of operating at a loss. A prolonged period of low prices will reduce him to bankruptcy. Space is against him.

The cost in social services

In recent years this gloomy economic picture has been somewhat altered by the development of highly mobile rubbertired farm machinery and the expansion of shipment by truck. But even when marketing problems resulting from geographic isolation are met, there remain other problems which are just as destructive of the morale and standards of the isolated family. Such families are almost bound to suffer in terms of social services available to them. They can scarcely hope to have adequate schools—and this is true of the isolated mining hamlet or textile village as well as of the isolated farm family. There are not enough pupils available to provide material for an adequately graded school. Even where economic return in terms of salary and living quarters for teachers is high—and it is almost always pitiably low—the isolation from cultural advantages and the lack of general social contacts make it difficult to secure teachers who can challenge young people with the real substance of education.

Consolidation is often suggested as the way out, but this carries with it other social costs. Isolated people live off the highway. If dependable transportation to consolidated schools is to be furnished, there must be all-weather roads maintained and kept open through all seasons of the year. And this faces the ordinary county or state government with costs so large as to render consolidation impractical. Under such circumstances, the old district school system continues with teachers salvaged for the most part from the residue of those left unemployed by more effective school systems.

Inadequate educational facilities and programs are only the beginning; such isolated families must do without telephone and electricity because of the high cost of supplying and maintaining such services when only a few families are using them. Health services are likewise available for the most part only at prohibitive costs. Doctors make their charges on a mileage basis and so are not called by the isolated family. And when the doctor does come, his help is rendered less effective because of the absence of those hospital facilities for diagnosis and treatment on which he has been taught to depend. It costs the people more to call the doctor; it costs him more to answer the call; inadequate resources limit his efficiency.

Hardship for the church

Nowhere does the isolated settler suffer more than in the difficulty he meets in his church program. Distance places greatly increased charges upon the slender resources available for the maintenance of the church. Northern Wisconsin gives us a rather typical picture of the effect on the church of isolated living. There farmers are living on scattered areas of good land in the midst of the scrub left in the wake of loggers' axes. They are few and widely dispersed, so that when they congregate to organize a church, they must travel long distances over poor roads to gather even a small membership. Within the West Wisconsin Conference of The Methodist Church, the Northern District contains the area of cutover counties with scattered and isolated settlement. When compared with other districts and the conference as a whole, the Northern District clearly shows its disadvantaged position.

Table IV on page 63 clearly shows the penalties which excess space puts upon church members and upon the program of the church. It costs more per member to maintain a church program; the pastor receives less for his services, even though his people pay more. An undue proportion of untrained pastors is found in this particularly needy field. As isolation increases, church members pay more and more for less and less, because of the sheer inefficiency of operating with small numbers of people.

TABLE IV

Comparisons of Districts of the West Wisconsin Conference on
Specific Economic and Social Indices (1953)

INDEX	WHOLE CONFERENCE	SOUTHERN DISTRICT	CENTRAL DISTRICT	NORTHERN DISTRICT
Per Capita Cost of Pastor's Salary ....$	7.91	$ 7.20	$ 8.03	$ 8.82
Pastor's Average Cash Salary	2,463.68	2,490.36	2,461.00	2,434.34
Members Served per Pastor	312	346	307	276
Percentage of Pastors Not Conf. Members ...	46.2	39.6	41.3	59.1

What is true on a district basis is also noticeable within a district. Within the Northern District a comparison may be made among areas of progressively sparser settlement. Table V below reveals the same forces at work. People pay more and more for less and less in the church as isolation increases.

TABLE V

Comparisons of Counties Within the Northern District on
Specific Economic and Social Indices (1953)

INDEX	NORTHERN DISTRICT	BARRON COUNTY (40.1 persons per sq. mile)	RUSK COUNTY (18.5 persons per sq. mile)	ASHLAND-BAYFIELD COUNTIES (13.2 persons per sq. mile)
Per Capita Cost of Pastor's Salary ....$	8.82	$ 8.67	$ 9.71	$ 9.81
Pastor's Average Cash Salary	2,434.34	2,982.00	1,955.67	1,563.33
Members Served per Pastor	276	344	201	159

Indeed, all the increased costs do not appear in the picture, for the people must travel great distances to attend church meetings, and the pastor must travel equally great distances to minister to his people. The per-capita-cost and average-salary figures do not reflect these additional charges against already depleted resources.

From the foregoing it seems fair to conclude that, under conditions of terrain and climate such as we have in northern Wisconsin, whenever the population density falls to a figure as low as thirteen per square mile—as it does in Ashland and Bayfield counties—we have a missionary situation for the church. Numbers are so few, distances are so great, economic resources are so small, that it is not reasonable to expect local people to defray the costs of an effective ministry. Yet these people, because of their very isolation, need more than other groups the morale-sustaining care of the church. Their courageous efforts to maintain churches in the face of every discouragement are the best evidence of their need. The whole church owes to these people the best talent in leadership and the best tools of service it can secure. In our missionary work we must now begin to discover such situations as are permanently missionary in character and to bring to them, not a temporary or year-to-year support, but a statesmanlike approach with permanent financial undergirding. The whole church should bear its share of the total costs which too much space lays upon the isolated settler.

5

LAND: BREAD AND BUTTER

THE FIRST comers to America were looking for silver and gold; these were the wealth the new lands had to offer. And there were gold and silver to be found, both stores of these metals already laid up by the inhabitants of the strange new country and unappropriated stores yet to be discovered and brought back to Europe. But the new lands had other wealth to give to those who came on a more patient quest. Settlers and colonists followed on the heels of the adventurers, and they found forests for building and fuel, meadows, and natural grasses for pasturage and hay, a soil with an almost magical productivity once preconceived European methods of agriculture had been given up for those learned from the native Indians, and a supply of wild game to provide subsistence for the settler until his fields and flocks came into production. More important than these specific riches, however, was the belief which speedily developed in their limitless extent. Although explorers gradually discovered the limits of the new country, the ordinary citizen subscribed to the myth of its endless and inexhaustible resources. "There is always more," he might have phrased his credo with regard to the American land.

Land enough for all

Early American economic life and social arrangements were based upon plentiful natural resources: men were scarce, natural wealth abundant. In the face of new and richer lands always westward there was no need to conserve the soil's fertility or prevent its loss through erosion by wind and weather. The southern planter could always take his slaves and move to the cheap lands westward, leaving the old, worn-out fields to grow up in brush and weeds. The New England farmer could turn from his hill acres, with their soil already growing thin, to the rich expanses of the Mohawk Valley and the forests and prairies of the old Northwest.

So it was not only with agricultural land but with other natural wealth. Cut down the trees for fuel or for lumber, or burn them to clear the land; there were always more forests to the west. Burn the gas in great torches in the streets at night; there was always more in the rich earth. Take the best of the coal or ore from the mine in such a way that the remainder was permanently rendered unavailable; there would be bigger and better mines farther west. Attitudes toward natural resources which were effective, necessary, and appropriate to a small band of settlers clinging to the rocky east coast of a vast and untamed continent were carried over and became the motivating force in the lives of the men and women who overran the continent. The myth of infinite and inexhaustible natural wealth governed the lives of rural Americans.

And within the limits of 2½ centuries the myth was truth. From the settlement at Jamestown into the 1880's there was abundant natural wealth for all. This plenty was an important basis of American egalitarianism and democracy. A man of force and courage need not be at the mercy of an unjust employer. He could go west and take up a homestead on free land. Twenty years of discipline and labor would make him a man of property and position, a man able to educate his children and provide for them a reasonable heritage. True, as he pierced the western prairies, he was met by drought that turned him back again and again; even when the miraculous earth turned forth crops of fabulous proportions, prices were so low and transportation costs so high that his apparent wealth melted away. But for the patient the rains always came, and then the desert blossomed as the rose. Eventually leaders rose to attack the railroads and to give the farmer a voice in the setting of agricultural prices. And there was always the good earth beyond, 160 acres to be had as a homestead if a man would live upon them and bring them into cultivation. A man could always be free so long as there was the land.

The end of free land

Then the land ran out. By 1890 all but occasional bits of the good lands were gone. Deserts remained, mountain wildernesses remained, there were acreages to be brought under irrigation, but fertile fields ready to produce no longer existed for the taking. Men had to live with what they had without the illusion of an inexhaustible frontier to comfort them. And with a dawning consciousness that the land of opportunity was gone, there began to develop an uneasy awareness that other resources had been lost along the way. Men began to see— first a few leaders, then bit by bit men everywhere—that certain of our natural resources cared for, conserved, might have proved to be an inexhaustible source of wealth and well-being, but that these same resources had been squandered and lost— in some cases irretrievably.

It was this discovery that brought into existence the conservation movement, of which President Theodore Roosevelt was so eloquent and effective a protagonist. It meant a change from slashing down whole forests to sustained-yield cutting of timber with the emphasis on use and replacement at an equal rate. It meant fish and game laws for both the amateur and the professional, in order to maintain and eventually to increase the stock of wildlife so dangerously depleted. It meant the use of mineral resources with a due regard for the national welfare, including the setting aside of strategic reserves against days of national emergency. But it meant most of all, and most important of all, a conservation of the soil out of which all other resources may be produced.

With this whole emphasis the Christian church has an innate

and immediate sympathy. We have never quite forgotten that our relationship to nature's gifts is one of stewardship, that we hold our dominion over the earth, not in fee simple, but in trust to God. God's injunction to us is: "Be fruitful, and multiply, and replenish the earth, and subdue it: and have dominion over the fish of the sea, and over the fowl of the air, and over every living thing that moveth upon the earth." What we are to have is *dominion,* not *destruction;* we are to *replenish,* not to *deplete.* The business of church and minister is to call our people to a sense of their trusteeship of the land under God. No farmer is a safe custodian of the soil for his generation until he has come to a conscious sense of his vocation as "working together with God."

Losing our soil

The threat to the soil against which the church must array itself is twofold: soil depletion and soil erosion. The first is the less serious threat, for soil fertility lost may always be replaced over a period of years. The loss of fertility temporarily removes land from useful cultivation and may actually spell ruin for the family cultivating that particular piece of land, for in the short run one-crop agriculture and careless tillage practices may reduce the productivity of land below a rate that will return a living to a family. But conservation practices can bring back into rich production neglected areas. It is the total loss of the soil through erosion which is most to be feared; for, when the soil is gone, it is gone until the slow geologic processes through thousands of years can build up a new soil—gone forever so far as our particular culture is concerned.

Erosion is of two kinds: by wind and by water. In dry lands the wind whips the soil away, but an overabundance of water may have precisely the same effect. The carrying power of both wind and water is not simply doubled when its velocity is doubled; carrying power increases at a much more rapid rate. Bare soil exposed without protection to high wind or running water will be caught up and borne away until the wind or water loses its high velocity and the soil is dumped in a new location. Control lies in both cases in providing the soil with an adequate cover which will resist the loosening of soil particles. In the case of water erosion an equally important problem is that of keeping the water on and in the soil, where it will promote plant growth. Wind erosion with tremendous dust storms is probably the more impressive form, but water erosion is, in the United States, the more extensive and destructive type. To it we shall give our particular attention.

Under wild conditions in nature, forest and bush or grass cover the soil and protect it from the ravages of both wind and rain. Not only is the soil not left bare to the streaming waters, but the plant growth impedes the course of the water as it comes down in rain and holds it in place until it has time to sink into the soil to supply the moisture for growth. Anyone who has spent a period in the forest knows that the trees drip for a day or more after the rain and that pools of water are gathered in stump holes, behind fallen trees, or in the hollows formed by the great surface roots. Some of the rain does run off immediately, of course; but even this small amount carries no soil with it, for the earth is covered not only by growing vegetation but also by the pine needles or decaying leaves which always carpet the forest floor. In prairie lands the same function is served by the lush growth of grasses and flowers. Their roots hold the soil in place; their foliage protects it from the pelting rain; their debris covers the earth and makes an absorbent carpet to hold the moisture for the soil. Erosion as a problem of soil loss begins when men strip the hills of their forests and break the grasslands with the plow. Then the natural balance of plant and weather and soil is broken, and the water begins to carry the soil downstream from the fields of the farmer.

What happens when soil begins to leave the fields and go downstream? First of all, the farmer becomes aware that he has lost the basic wealth out of which all his other wealth must grow. His fields begin to show thin spots of soil; their fertility decreases. Worst of all, gullies begin to form, which cut back through fields, destroying their usefulness, though good soil be left upon them, by making cultivation difficult and uneconomical. And gullies do not stay at home. Here I am most emphatically my brother's keeper and he mine. For my gully cuts back across his eighty; nothing will stop it at the line fence; and my gully cuts across the township road which our common taxes maintain. Soon my careless cultivation, my refusal to regard the soil as God's sacred trust to me, has set loose upon my neighborhood and community an eating cancer, destroying whole fields and setting charges for roads, bridges, culverts, against the whole countryside.

Downstream costs of erosion

So much is bad, but that is only the beginning—the loss of the soil from my field. What I lose, someone else must receive. Down the stream the soil goes until the current slackens, when the river or creek reaches some power dam or harbor installation. There the soil is deposited to silt up the reservoir, to make a new bar in the way of river traffic, to demand expensive dredging operations to keep the channels open. What was once my wealth becomes now someone else's burden, a charge on wealth, private and public. Even though it silts up no reservoir or harbor, it still fills up the stream bed and renders the river more likely to overflow its banks and flood the fields and villages nearby when the spring rains and thaw bring the flood currents downstream next year.

But, someone urges, the river sometimes overflows the bottom lands and deposits the rich soil on farmers' fields there. The upstream farmer has lost, but the downstream farmer has gained, so that there is no total loss to the society as a whole. It is true, of course, that a small proportion of the soil is deposited where it can be used again, so that not so much is lost. Unfortunately erosion continues when the soil has gone. The rains will carry gravel and rubble as well as good soil, and they will deposit refuse and trash on the downstream fields as quickly as they will good soil. Connecticut River bottom farmers in Massachusetts and Connecticut rejoiced in the annual increments to their onion and tobacco fields which came down the river from the acres of Vermont; but floods in the thirties began to bring down gravel and deposit it upon the rich fields, and then the downstream farmers began to sense the total importance of soil conservation everywhere. In the long run, erosion anywhere along a river system means problems everywhere along that system. The Tennessee Valley Authority is our first national effort to meet the land problem of a whole river system by a united plan and program.

Even now we have not detailed all the costs of failure to practice soil conservation. Eroding lands promote a rapid runoff when the rains come. Water which should sink into the soil to replenish underground water supplies quickly runs off along the surface. When the summer drought comes, the water is not there to provide the roots with their extra supply. Instead of being released gradually into the brooks, creeks, and rivers, it goes off all at once. Such a sudden discharge of water means floods downstream, higher levees and river walls, the continual threat of destruction to cities and towns along the river, and all the higher public and private costs that go with facing and fighting a flood menace.

Conservation of the soil simply means a program of agriculture which seeks to keep the soil on the land and the water in the soil. It not only enriches the individual farmer but enriches all his fellow citizens within the watershed. Soil conservation means cheaper electricity, cheaper transportation, lower taxes, lives safe from the threat of flood. It is the American farmer's best opportunity for loyal service to the nation and the world. Thousands of farmers following good soil practices are engaged in what may pass for a very prosaic task, but their efforts are fraught with dramatic meaning for all Americans both now and in the future.

United States Soil Conservation Service

The nation has approached the problem of eroding soils through the United States Soil Conservation Service within the Department of Agriculture. The Soil Conservation Service operates through democratically established and governed Soil Conservation Districts. This service stands ready to offer to farmers advisory counsel in soil-conserving practices and to help them band together collectively for common action within a locality in meeting peculiar local problems. Soil-conserving practices include such procedures as putting into permanent forest the steeper hillsides, plowing and planting all crops on the contour, terracing of some fields, strip planting of others, and the development of permanent pasture. It is the duty of the Christian pastor to be informed about soil conditions as they affect his section of the country and to be able to refer his parishioners to the appropriate office of the Soil Conservation Service. He can secure such information by a letter to the United States Soil Conservation Service, Department of Agriculture, Washington, D. C., if he cannot discover a local Soil Conservation District office near at hand.

And the pastor in securing this advice for his people is not acting without regard for his own and the church's welfare. A study was made in 1939-41 of 222 rural churches in South Carolina by Dr. Buie of the Soil Conservation Service. Table VI below gives the results. In each case the church suffered with

TABLE VI

Selected Indices on 222 Rural Churches in South Carolina—1939, 1940, 1941

TYPE OF EROSION	NO. OF CHURCHES	NO. OF MEMBERS	GIFTS TO MISSIONS	SUPPORT OF PASTORS	SUNDAY-SCHOOL CONTRIBUTIONS
Moderate 47	160	$71.28	$431.37	$126.11
Moderate to Severe ..89	132	49.47	299.93	69.59
Severe 86	105	31.23	241.09	50.50

the land. And the church suffered because people were suffering. Poor land means land from which farm families can get at best only a scanty living. Such land gives a poor tax base on which to support schools. Thus the church has not only less in the way of financial resources in such areas but has to depend on weaker families and poorer schools for that fundamental discipline of personality on which it builds for God's kingdom.

The minister and the church must stand for the conservation of land in every way. As stewards we must care for God's gifts; as socially concerned persons we must husband our lands for the sake of others; as social technicians we must secure an adequate economic base for home, school, and church. From every point of view we are called to a crusade for the holy earth.

6

LAND: YOURS AND MINE

LAND IS space, and land is natural wealth. In each of these senses land makes special problems and opportunities for persons and therefore for the church and its pastor. But land is something more: it is somebody's land. It has an owner; it is subject to control by and use under a social institution—property. And this is universally true wherever men and women live a settled life. What property in land involves varies greatly from country to country and culture to culture, but there is always a socially accredited system for the use of land which conditions to a notable extent the life of the people whose system it is.

Most of the immigrants who peopled North America came from countries in which land was entailed and a system of primogeniture governed inheritance. Entailed land ownership means that land is owned by a family and not an individual. An individual has the use of the land during his lifetime, but he cannot dispose of it permanently; he must conserve it and turn it over intact to the family representative in the next generation upon his own death. With a system of entail is often—indeed, almost universally among Europeans—associated a system of primogeniture—that is, inheritance by the first-born, generally the first-born son. When entail and primogeniture are associated, they provide for a consistent stewardship of the land and the maintenance of the family name. Unfortunately they do not provide for growing families; they leave the younger sons at loose ends. And this is particularly true in an agricultural economy, where the fundamental means of making a living is the land. Where land cannot be bought, where land always stays in the family and with the eldest son, the lot of younger sons is precarious and unhappy.

Fee-simple ownership of the land

North America was settled by younger sons. Like all generalizations, this one is open to serious attack; but it is certainly true that the point of view conditioning the development of ideas about property in the United States was the point of view of the younger son, hungry for the economic opportunity denied him by Old World institutions. Here was plenty of land, and he intended to have some. Further, he intended that *all his* sons should have land, that land should be as nearly free as it was possible to make it. And it seemed to him that the way to bring about this laudable result was to develop a conception of property in land as contrary to European conceptions as it was possible to make it. Consequently he developed the holding of land in fee-simple ownership; that is, land became a commodity freely traded like other commodities. The early American did not ask if this sort of ownership was suited to the nature of land. He simply insisted that land should be made available to all persons on a free-market basis.

Such a system of property in land has certain results that follow from it absolutely. One of the most important is that land becomes subject to advancing and declining prices like any other commodity; in other words, speculation in land becomes possible. And speculation in land means that land may be taken up, not for purposes of cultivation, but for immediate resale on a rising market. American land settlement from the establishment of the public domain until the passage of the Homestead Act in Lincoln's first term was a long series of skirmishes between bona fide settlers on the one hand and speculators on the other. The passage of the Homestead Act resolved the struggle, nominally at least, in favor of the settler, but speculators were still able to secure public lands through one subterfuge or another and thus to bid up the price of land.

A second unanticipated result was that a farm was required to pay for itself once in every generation. A farmer who had homesteaded his land and reared a family of six children was faced, as he became old, with the problem of what to do with his land. Perhaps his eldest son was ready to take over the farm, but that left five other children to provide for out of the parental estate. To give the farm to the oldest boy would be unfair to the others, according to American ways of thinking; and so the farm was sold to the oldest boy, and a mortgage was taken by the other five children for their five sixths of the property. The son operating the property was then forced so to operate it that it would not only maintain him and his family but would also pay five sixths of its cash value to his brothers and sisters over a lifetime. Thus a farm was required to pay for itself once in every generation.

As long as speculative rises in the price of land occurred with regularity, the increase in capital value of a farm could be counted on to pay for that farm. A boy who bought a farm from his father at a price of twenty-five dollars an acre could sell when he became an old man at fifty dollars an acre and thus get the full purchase price back again beyond his own investment. But such a process is self-limiting. It can go on for two or three generations at the most. Then the land has become worth more than it will produce, and instead of an increase in the price per acre the owner must expect a slump. In the long run this system of land ownership in fee simple has not provided more land for more people as it was hoped, but has seen the gradual reduction of land ownership by the working farmer.

Trends in tenancy

Table VII on page 77 gives the picture of what has happened. It was pointed out in the previous chapter that at about the year 1880 free land was gone. From 1880 until 1930 the percentage of farms operated by tenants increased for each ten-year period. Since 1930 the proportion of tenants has steadily decreased. This is due to a variety of factors. Governmental policies have made credit resources available to working farmers. A high level of prices for farm products has enabled mortgaged owners to pay off indebtedness on their property and tenants to purchase property of their own. Increasing mechanization has reduced materially the number and proportion of cropper farmers in the South. It appears that the recent farm prosperity has been wisely used by many farm families to undergird their permanent investment in land. Farm policy, both governmental and private, should be geared to maintaining and continuing the use of farm wealth to make the individual farm family independent on the land. A marked reduction in the relative price level of agricultural products would be most unfortunate so far as land ownership and tenure are concerned.

TABLE VII

Percentage of U. S. Farms Operated by Tenants

YEAR	PERCENTAGE OF FARMS OPERATED BY TENANTS
1880	25.6
1890	28.4
1900	35.3
1910	37.0
1920	38.1
1930	42.4
1940	38.7
1945	31.7
1950	26.7

Tenancy may be good

Perhaps, however, tenancy is not such a bad thing after all. Is it necessarily true that the man who owns his own land is better off than the man who rents land from another? Many of us know thrifty renters whose standard of living and standard of life are higher than those of neighboring owners who are rotting out spiritually and mentally on their ancestral acres. Before we can evaluate tenancy in the large, we must understand what it means. There is not just one thing called tenancy, but there are several related ways of holding land, all of which are classified under this common head.

Tenancy is sometimes the second or third step a boy takes on the ladder which leads from being a hired hand to owning a farm for himself. He has amassed a little capital; he has acquired some stock by working on shares with his employer. He is now ready to start out for himself. But he is not ready either to pay for the land he is to operate or—and this is important—to decide what piece of land best suits him for a permanent family setting. He puts his capital into machinery and tools and moves his stock to a rented farm—perhaps a farm now or soon to be on the market—which he is considering buying. The institution of tenancy permits him to apply his meager capital as efficiently as possible and offers him a chance to try the farm before he buys it. Tenancy at this level has decided advantages. In general, tenancy which permits the tenant to operate the land with independence and ingenuity, which makes him secure in the enjoyment of improvements he introduces to the farm, which does not relegate him and his family to a low social status in community affairs, and which is a doorway to future increasing independence—such tenancy must be regarded as socially valuable.

Much tenancy is bad

Much tenancy, however, is not of this type. The sharecropper, for example, furnishes his labor and operates his land virtually under the dictatorship of the landlord. This system of land operation destroys his independence and imagination, as it requires of him only obedience and labor. Because his imagination is not given scope in his daily toil, it is continually seeking a happier future in a different setting. He always wants to move—to the next county, to the next state. Studies in Georgia show that one third of the sharecroppers move every year. And because he always is on the move mentally, he is not concerned for a better house where he is, for better fields and finer crops. His operation of land is conditioned by an impermanence of outlook which causes him to be indifferent to erosion and the loss of soil fertility. After all, he is not going to be here next year.

His sense of impermanence leads him to a relative indifference to the social life of his community. Why work in the church or attend its services when he will probably not be near this church next year? Children moved from school to school at frequent intervals acquire at best only a thin whitewash of education. Ideals and values from community institutions have little chance to find soil and take vital root. Religiously the sharecropper turns to the peripatetic revivalist who serves up for his starved imagination a vivid and materialistic imagery. He has no church; his religious concern is exhausted in the emotional excesses induced by the fly-by-night religious speculator. The net picture we get when we examine this sort of tenancy is that of eroding soil, eroding people, eroding institutions. The sands of life are running out for a culture which tolerates such handling of its soil.

It is probably safe to say that wherever more than half the land or land value is operated by persons who do not own it, the type of tenancy developed is an unhealthy one. This is an arbitrary figure, but it indicates that owners, as they grow old and retire, are not being replaced by other owners. The percentage of tenancy might run much higher than this—as it does in England, for example—and still not threaten either the soil or the men on the soil and their institutions, but only provided that tenants are secure in their operations and given scope for imaginative management and the enjoyment of the benefits accruing therefrom. As yet our American tenure arrangements do not provide such security.

Under American conditions, when the percentage of tenancy

rises beyond fifty per cent, certain associated factors begin to operate. Large-scale land holdings develop, or at least large-scale management of holdings of absentee owners. And with such large-scale ownership or operation there arises a demand for farm labor, much of which, because of the seasonal nature of so much farm work, is migrant labor. The migrant laborer has always been at the bottom of the social pyramid in American life. Originally migrant laborers were almost exclusively men. But the last twenty years have seen the rise of a class of family migrants throughout the United States. John Steinbeck in *The Grapes of Wrath* dramatized the plight of such families in California. But the problems posed in his novel have a much wider currency than California. Patterns of migration extend up and down both west and east coasts of the United States. Migrants move up from Texas through Arkansas and Missouri to the strawberry fields of southern Illinois and the orchards of Michigan and Wisconsin; others swing through the wheat fields from Texas to Canada. There are few agricultural states that do not entertain these homeless families for some part of the season.

The migrant on the land

What we have said of the plight of the sharecropper applies to an even greater extent to the migrant. A visitor in southern Illinois during the strawberry-picking season found there a family that had had no permanent home for thirteen years. Think what it means to be thirteen years without a settled residence—without a vote, without a home town, without a school, without a church. In the light of such a case, Christians must ask themselves how large a proportion of migrants we can tolerate within the social fabric without destruction of the fabric itself. The church is concerned here not simply with the plight of persons who receive in return for their arduous labor few, if any, of those social services and rewards which are the essence of a cultured life; the church is concerned with a condition which, if long continued, will make all cultured life impossible.

The *1943 National Convocation on the Church in Town and Country* had this to say regarding our responsibility to migrants:

To establish a stable society in the postwar period it is essential for the Church to encourage and support government and private agencies in action leading toward (a) farm ownership for the low income families; (b) the publishing of factual information as to labor needs each year in the different crop areas; (c) the establishment of minimum healthful standards of housing and medical attention; (d) the regulation of child labor and the protection of the rights of migrants to collective bargaining. Such goals will only be achieved upon the basis of helping the migrant to make full use of his own creative abilities.

The Christian Church should effectively lend its support to practical, economical efforts upon the part of the government and private agencies to meet the needs of migratory peoples. . . .

The immediate responsibility is a program of Christian social service to meet the physical, moral, social, and spiritual needs of the migrants. It has a special responsibility to furnish the spiritual motivation which will assist the migrant in living life day by day on worthwhile terms.

Some of the features of such a program of Christian social service should be:

1. A study of the specific problems and needs of migrants in a given area.
2. The establishment of personal contacts between residents and migrants through which favorable community attitudes might be created.
3. The creating of opportunities for group fellowship between residents and migrants.
4. Assisting the migrant and his employer to understand each other's problems.
5. Acquainting key people in government and private agencies with the needs of migrants and encouraging them to make available their particular resources.

At the same time the Church has a long-range responsibility for preventing migrancy and for helping migrants to re-establish themselves in a community. The following steps should be taken toward the achievement of this end:

1. Helping potential migrants to remain on the land and to own their own farms.
2. Vocational training to assist migrants in adding to their productive ability.
3. The resettlement of migrants on subsistence acreages with opportunities for seasonal agricultural employment.
4. The establishment of co-operative farms in areas where industrialized farming is an established practice, so that the farmer may have under such conditions a stake in the land.
5. The planning for combination of opportunities for seasonal industrial and seasonal agricultural employment.

Ten years later the same convocation, meeting in St. Paul, had this to say:

There are many reasons for the use of migratory labor in this country. Some of these reasons are: short-term tenancy, the need for "cheap labor," and the demand for seasonal labor beyond that which can be supplied from local sources.

Changes in our diet have brought a greater demand for fruits and vegetables. With new and larger machinery, the farmer operator can plant much more than he alone can harvest. These are some of the factors which contribute to the increased demand for migratory agricultural labor.

Before World War I, laborers moved relatively short distances to harvest crops. Then came a depression which threw these people into a situation of unemployment, thus migrating greater distances in search of work, even at starvation wages.

What can the Church do? The commission was agreed that the church should work for such agricultural and industrial policies as will lessen the need for migratory labor. Where it is found to be necessary the church should prepare the community for the arrival of the workers, encourage improvement of housing, sanitation, education, and the general living and working condition of the migrants.

The church should accept its obligation to minister physically, spiritually and educationally to these people. It should participate in educational campaigns to help communities and the migrants themselves to raise their standards of living.

In relation to low-income families, it should be the purpose and objective of the church to teach abundant living, which includes not only spiritual values but also cleanliness and a worthy use of leisure time.

In cut-over timber areas, the church should encourage more diversified farming so far as climate permits. Auxiliary seasonal industry should also be encouraged.

In relation to mountain folk, the church should bring the gospel of more abundant living to these people at the level of their own language and religious interest.

The need for informative and helpful literature along these lines is urgent. It should be directed to employers and migratory laborers, alike.

Implicit in this discussion, though not stated, is the demand that migrancy makes upon the society which tolerates it. Migrants receiving a very meager income are almost sure to become public charges at the slightest dislocation of the pattern of work and travel upon which they depend. Undernourished and poorly housed, they are an easy prey to disease of all kinds, and they may carry contagion from one community to the next. Poorly schooled, their children become a handicap to other children on the few occasions when they do enter a public school for a little space of learning. Their limitations prevent the teacher from making the progress with the class which other children could follow.

Such a situation means that migrants are seldom wanted in any role in the community save that of casual worker. Once the work is done, settled citizens hope and expect that the migrant will move on. His presence among them as anything but a worker is a burden and a blight, and they often treat him in this light. The result is the building up of resentments within the migrant group and the creation in certain migrants of a sense that moral obligations do not hold for people who show toward them so little respect and appreciation. The charge often leveled against migrants that they have no moral standards, that they are dishonest and tricky, is a reflection of the outcast position in which the migrant finds himself and to which he reacts by such retaliatory behavior as will damage those who so despise him.

How the church can help

In this chapter we have outlined three sets of problems: (1) problems of the debt-ridden owner of land, (2) problems of the renter, and (3) problems of the farm laborer, particularly the migrant. To these three sets of problems, which have their common focus in the relationship of man to the land, there is no simple and easy solution. When we further complicate the picture by pointing out that the problems vary with type of land, type of climate, and type of crops, we can readily understand that there is to the problem no single solution which the church ought to support. What the church must do is strive for a recognition of the human values involved in all situations and problems.

Self-sufficiency and diversification in farming

In general, all agricultural workers would be better off if they would strive for a greater degree of self-sufficiency in agriculture. The pastor who can encourage his people not to trust in a cash crop exclusively but to raise a garden, keep poultry and a cow, perhaps raise a litter of pigs, has put his people on the road to a way of life which will make them increasingly independent of the ups and downs of our total commercial economy.

Again, we may safely hazard that all farmers would be better off in planning a diversified program of crops rather than in following a one-crop system. Diversification permits crop rotation and better soil practice, and in addition gives the farmer several commodities to market, so that if prices are low on one, he still may do well on another. There are, of course, soils and climates that do not favor diversification, but the burden of proof should rest upon a one-crop system of agriculture, since such a system does put the farmer so much at the mercy of the market.

Church homestead plans

Beyond these two general suggestions, the pastor in an area of family-sized farms may help his young people to secure farms of their own. Calvin Schnucker, formerly pastor at Titonka, Iowa, now professor at Dubuque Theological Seminary, developed such a program with great success. He began by preaching to his young people the importance of farming as a way of life, the need for thrift if one was to purchase a farm, the need for scientific training if one was to operate a farm with success. Meanwhile he interviewed banks and insurance companies with holdings within the area of his parish to determine what they had for sale and what their prices were. Next he went over the available farms with the county agent to establish whether they were fairly priced or not. Finally, when a boy had something set aside with which to purchase a place, his pastor took him to see banker and county agent to find just the sort of place he wanted and could use. The pastor's good word enabled the boy to receive credit terms much more generous than he might otherwise have secured. In this situation the pastor served as a center for motivation and information and guaranteed the character of the young man to the seller. In six years the percentage of owner-operated land within the parish rose from 34 to 60 per cent. Incidentally, during the same six years the budget of the church tripled.

The Methodist Church has provided in its official machinery for the Farm and Home Committee in a local church. The purpose of this committee is to assist young couples in finding and securing farms or small-business opportunities within the community. *The Rural Lutheran,* published by a Lutheran Inter-synodical Editorial Board with offices at 200 South Fifth Street, Blair, Nebraska, carries a series of advertisements under the heading "placement service," to help young Lutheran couples to find places to establish themselves economically in Lutheran church neighborhoods. Local churches in many cases have explored local and federal credit sources and have called to the attention of their young people the sources of help available to them. In the Lagrange County Larger Parish (Indiana) the Farm and Home Committee has helped five young couples to secure the services of the Farmers' Home Administration in purchasing farms of their own.

Individual pastors have found that they have a ministry to farmers nearing the age of retirement in raising with them the Christian problem of what to do with the farm. A Christian steward seeks to make what he has disclose what he is; he frames his farm operations to the glory of God, because he recognizes himself as a son of God. But when he leaves his farm, who will continue the stewardship he has carried over the years? It is the retiring farmer's responsibility to see to it that his successor brings to that special bit of ground the same love and devotion which he has bestowed upon it; otherwise all his care over the years may be destroyed in a few years of exploitation. The pastor can often suggest young men who would make worthy successors in such a Christian stewardship when a farmer's own children do not wish to succeed him. From his state extension service he can secure materials on leasing arrangements and contract plans whereby a farm can be transferred from the older man to the younger with fairness to each. Such assistance to both the old and the young is a real pastoral challenge.

Finally, wherever tenancy now exists, the pastor of the church must strive for better relationships between landlord and tenant. Both must be made to see that their mutual relationship to the land is not something private and personal but is a relationship fraught with highest significance for the public good. Their arrangements with each other in leasing and working the land must be such as provide for the land that stable care and permanent conservation which it needs. Only as we conserve the soil do we have any right either as landlord or as tenant to the fruits of the soil. What we get at the price of soil depletion and soil erosion is a plain theft from the generations that succeed us and from our neighbors whose land suffers a like fate with our own.

7

IN UNION STRENGTH

LAND, THE economic base on which rural life rests, has several meanings, and associated with each meaning is a complex
of special problems which are the concern of the church and
the minister because they profoundly affect the welfare not only
of men upon the land but of the whole body politic. These
problems have not arisen in a moment, nor without reaction
on the part of rural people. They are problems of economic
support which people over a long period of time have attempted
to meet through organization. Most of us are familiar with the
end products of such organization within the rural community.
We may belong to the Grange or some other rural organization
and yet not sense that its fundamental reason for existence lies
in problems related to land. In this chapter we shall discuss
several of these rural organizations, for they represent attitudes
toward fundamental values within rural life in which the
church too has a stake. These organizations are a part of the
total life of America, however, and it should be obvious that
in a single chapter we can scarcely do justice to their history
or their programs.

The earliest rural organizations to face these problems in the
United States were agricultural societies which sponsored county
fairs. Their main function was educational, bringing to the attention of farmers new methods of tillage, new tools, new crops,
new strains of seed, new breeds of livestock, and new systems of
crop rotation. To this educational function was soon added an

attempt at motivation through the offering of prizes and awards for quality products. Education and motivation naturally developed a demand for a commercial element through which the farmer could make arrangements to purchase the new and better seeds or secure the breeding services of a sire for his flock or herd. This again opened the way to herd improvement, the standardization of breeds, and all the careful animal husbandry that has given us our modern cattle, sheep, and swine.

The Grange

The Grange represents the first national attempt to organize rural people—in this case farmers—into a national organization for the purpose of redressing economic wrongs. It was founded in December of 1867 with the name "Patrons of Husbandry" by a little company of federal officeholders in Washington, D. C., under the leadership of Oliver H. Kelley. Mr. Kelley had been sent on a tour through the South after the War Between the States by President Johnson to survey and analyze the plight of southern agriculture. No record of any report of this trip exists, but the Grange is a monument to it, for Mr. Kelley returned home with two convictions: the first was that the economic condition of the farmer was so serious that some action must be taken in his favor; the second was that a fraternal organization would offer to the farmer the tool he needed to help himself.

Mr. Kelley, originally a Minnesota farmer, set out from Washington, after the establishment of the Patrons of Husbandry, to organize local Granges. His efforts met with so little success that he was forced ultimately to borrow money from a fellow Mason to reach his Minnesota home. There he settled to a life in which farming was mixed with periodic tours to organize Granges and a constant writing to the newspapers of letters describing the farmer's plight. Gradually, at first, and then with increased momentum the organization began to take hold. By 1869 it had become a force sweeping over the Northeast and the Middle West. By the year 1875 it was able to boast of 850,000 members.

The Grange was especially concerned with problems arising out of land as space. Farmers in the 1860's and '70's were isolated from stores and markets for the sale of their products. They were dependent on their local merchant, more or less forced to pay whatever he might charge, and had to sell their product at a faraway market and pay for its transportation pretty much whatever the railroad cared to charge. The Grange as a fraternal order stressed buying and selling together and made its chief attacks on the local retailer and the railroads. It suggested buying commodities as a group and offered plans whereby the local Grange secretary could place group orders with wholesale houses and distribute the goods to the Grange members at a marked saving to all. Out of this order system grew the Grange stores, originally organized as co-operatives. Many of these failed because farmers were not willing to pay a salary sufficient to secure well-trained help. Others that proved successful went into private hands, since they were organized as joint-stock companies and not under Rochdale principles with "one member, one vote" control. It was in large part the failure of these local business concerns which reduced the Grange membership to one eighth of its greatest size by 1879.

The most notable achievement of the Grange was the establishment of the principle of government control of public utilities. This arose out of the Grange attack on the railroads. Prior to this time the railroads had been their own law so far as rates and service were concerned. From their rulings, no matter how arbitrary they might seem to be, there was no appeal, since they alone connected the farmer with his market. The Grange made this matter a political issue and elected men to various state assemblies on the basis of their willingness to vote rate and schedule controls. Certain of the legislatures did vote such controls, some of them rather stringent. An appeal taken by the operator of a grain elevator in Chicago led the Supreme Court to declare the right of a state or the federal government to regulate a private business "affected by the public interest."

Though the Grange declined tremendously in membership after its first phenomenal growth, it never ceased to exist as an influential organization, and it has had a steady growth ever since its first and precipitate decline. In February, 1954, it reported 860,000 members in thirty-seven states. Its strength is centered in New England, New York, New Jersey, Pennsylvania, Ohio, Idaho, Washington, and Oregon. Its local organization is theoretically a township unit; above the local Grange are "Pomona Grange," theoretically a county unit, and the state and national Granges. The order makes much of social and educational programs in connection with the local Granges. It contains, particularly in New England, a large membership of village people who are not farmers at all. Its chief farm influence at present is through the pressure of its Washington lobby on national agricultural legislation and policy.

The Farmers' Alliance

In terms of influence the Grange was succeeded by the Farmers' Alliance. This organization contrasted with the Grange at about every point. While the Grange was nationally established before even a single local group was founded, the Alliance had its beginning in several small local groups, branching out into state and then regional federations; at no time was there a single national Alliance. Whereas the Grange put much emphasis on ritual and fraternal considerations, the Alliance from the first placed little emphasis on the social side and was much concerned to secure governmental intervention and aid for the working farmer. The Alliance distrusted the banking and credit system, had its own favorite scheme for the establishment in every county of subtreasuries of the federal government where a farmer could store his produce and receive loans against its value, became more and more interested in a money system tied to commodities rather than gold, and eventually threw its strength behind the Populist movement in politics.

The subtreasury plan is an interesting anticipation of currently operated plans for lending farmers funds against their commodities and for an ever-normal granary. The strength of the Alliance was in the South and in the plain states; it never established itself with any strength in the Northeast. With the defeat of the Populists its power collapsed, and it ceased to exist on any influential national scale. A few local organizations of the Alliance still exist in Pennsylvania and hold an annual state convention. There may be vestiges of the organization still at work in other localities.

The Farmers' Educational and Co-operative Union

Newt Gresham, a Texas cotton farmer, established the Farmers' Educational and Co-operative Union in his home state in 1902. He and his fellow farmers who joined with him to constitute the new organization felt themselves to be the victims of low prices for cotton dictated by the cotton exchanges and the manufacturers. Their problem was therefore to develop some common plan whereby they could increase their own bargaining capacity in relationship to the cotton exchanges. Gresham was of the opinion that farmers could control the price of cotton if they agreed among themselves what price they would accept and held their cotton off the market until that price was offered. Beginning in 1904, the Union set a price for cotton— ten cents a pound—and instructed its members to refuse to sell their cotton until this price was offered. At first the price did not rise as Gresham predicted, but in 1906 the market price approximated the price set by the Union. Leaders soon saw that the supply available also affected prices offered and attempted in one year to get members of the organization to plow under a part of their crop. Some actually did plow under cotton, but it was not done to any effective extent. Holding cotton involved the farmers in problems in the solution of which the Union achieved its most effective leadership. If cotton is to be held, it must be stored; to help farmers hold their cotton, the Union developed its own co-operative warehouses and gins. It is in the field of co-operative processing and marketing of such crops as cotton and small grains that the Union has made its most effective contributions.

By 1908 the Union had reached a membership of more than 900,000, with its strength in the South and in the hundredth-meridian states. It developed co-operatives on a large scale, emphasized the importance of sampling and of grading of cotton and other commodities, established consumer co-operative services for its members—notably the Farmers' Union Exchange at Omaha, really a mail-order co-operative for Farmers' Union members—and developed increasing emphasis on the educational part of its official name.

Membership in the Farmers' Union is on the basis of dues paid by the head of the family. Wife and children belong automatically when the family joins. This membership, furthermore, is not a nominal matter but offers decided advantages to participants. Young people are organized into two auxiliaries: Junior Reserves, those from twelve to sixteen years of age; and Juniors, those from sixteen to twenty-one. Their program involves learning to work together and to develop a sense of morale and mutual responsibility as farm people, acquiring information and experience in co-operative techniques, and training and experience in organization and public speaking. Along with this goes a full program of recreation, with emphasis on developing real recreational skills in folk games, drama, hobbies, as well as just having a good time. Camps and conventions for youth help the local union to develop leadership in its young members.

On April 30, 1954, the Union reported 242,255 paid family memberships. Actual membership includes, of course, the individuals comprising the families, so that the "voting membership is estimated at well over 600,000." States with largest memberships are Alabama with 45,019 members and North Dakota with 41,415. Membership is reported for twenty-three states and two divisions, Eastern and Rocky Mountain. Perhaps the relatively small membership of the Farmers' Union as contrasted with other farm organizations is due to the insistence of the organization that membership should not be nominal but that members should study and learn to better their collective condition. As a result of this emphasis, members of the Union have been leaders in their communities in various radical attempts to improve the position of the farmer. The Farm Holiday Association, with its direct-action tactics, was led and developed by Farmers' Union men. Though the Association was never approved by the national Farmers' Union, several state unions did give it their endorsement, and Milo Reno, Iowa Union state president, served as national president of the Association.

In this connection it is only fair to note that certain of the leaders of the Union made common cause in 1936 with Father Coughlin and William Lemke in the abortive Union Party. The leadership which gave this support to Coughlin and Lemke was repudiated by the 1936 convention of the Farmers' Union and removed from office. Dissidents then withdrew from the Farmers' Union and set up a competing organization, the Farmers' Guild. This latter organization has had an insignificant history, marked by a steady decline in membership and influence. If it is still in existence, its influence now is purely a local one. The Farmers' Union, as such, repudiated any connection with Coughlin, Lemke, and the Union Party.

In national affairs the Farmers' Union can be counted on to take the side of the small farmer, the tenant, and the farm laborer. Recently the Union appointed a director of intergroup relations with responsibility for cultivating and maintaining "friendly, co-operative, and creative relations" with such groups as the following: "other liberal farm and commodity organizations; co-operatives and co-operative associations; labor organizations; religious organizations; educational organizations; political (nonpartisan) organizations."

The directive under which the director operates lists such lines of action as "personal contact and association with leaders among these groups," "invitations to and hospitality for leaders of these groups at Farmers' Union conventions," and "participation in co-operative action projects, jointly conceived, aimed at the attainment of common goals." Obviously the Union does not conceive of its function in narrowly occupational terms.

The American Farm Bureau Federation

The American Farm Bureau Federation, known generally as the Farm Bureau, originated under the sponsorship of the Agricultural Extension Service of the federal government. In connection with the Department of Agriculture campaign against the boll weevil in the South, Dr. S. Knapp appointed county agents of the department to instruct local farmers in control methods and to help them in their use. The employment of county agents spread to the North; the first agent was appointed in Bedford County, Pennsylvania, in 1910 and in Broome County, New York State, in 1911. New York State farmers, feeling that they ought to have a say in the work of this agent, established the first county Farm Bureau in 1913 to advise with and assist the agent in his work. The passage by Congress of the Smith-Lever Act in 1914 established a system whereby federal funds were available if matched by state or local funds for employment of county agents. In several states such local funds were raised by solicitation of farmers and others; the persons who paid fees for the support of the county agent were members of the Farm Bureau. Often these persons were not farmers but local businessmen, bankers, and professionals who wished to see the farmer helped. It should be emphasized that in its beginnings the Farm Bureau movement was not intended as a farmers' movement in the Grange or Alliance pattern but was strictly a practical means of securing the services of a trained agriculturalist for the farmers of a county.

County Farm Bureaus began to organize into state federations as early as 1915. In 1919 was organized the National Farm Bureau Federation, composed of the state federations then existing. With this state and national organization, the Farm Bureau became something more than the local support of a county agent. On the state level federations organized various co-operative purchasing and marketing associations to serve their county organizations and represented their constituents with the state governments in affairs involving agriculture. Increasingly the national federation has spoken for agriculture in political developments in Washington, D. C. In recent years it has lined up against the Farmers' Union on almost every matter affecting agriculture. While it is undoubtedly true that there are farmers of all classes in Farm Bureau membership, the national leaders speak for and represent large-scale commercial agriculture. A study of a thousand farm families in New York State indicated that 60 per cent of farm owners were members of the Farm Bureau, 6 per cent of farm tenants were members, and membership on the part of farm laborers was negligible. The Farm Bureau as a national farmers' movement is the voice of the big farming interests.

The basic unit of the Farm Bureau is the county Farm Bureau, however, and these units as well as the various state federations are independent and autonomous in relationship to the national federation. County units will often be found rendering excellent service to all farmers within their area, while state federations may represent an entirely different point of view from that of the national society. The Ohio Farm Bureau, to name the conspicuous example, under the leadership of Murray Lincoln, is an outstanding servant of all farmers in that state. In general it can be counted on to take a stand in opposition to the national organization. It has sponsored and encouraged consumers', as well as processing and marketing, co-operatives. Among its own members it has developed a far-reaching educational movement through neighborhood discussion groups.

The Farm Bureau reported 1,591,777 dues-paying members on January 1, 1954, and is thus the largest of the farmer organizations. There were members in all forty-eight states and Puerto Rico. Smallest membership of any state was Rhode Island with 212, and the largest was Illinois with 200,015. States with more than 50,000 members included Alabama, Arkansas,

California, Illinois, Indiana, Iowa, Kansas, Kentucky, Michigan, New York, North Carolina, and Texas. In some states, such as New York and Ohio, there is a considerable overlap of membership between Grange and Farm Bureau. In states where the Farm Bureau is the official local sponsor of the extension-service program and the county agent, this official position has given it an undue advantage over its rivals in recruiting membership. Particularly in the South in the early days of the AAA program, crop-curtailment and soil-conservation checks were paid at the county agent's office at the same time that dues for membership in the Farm Bureau were being collected. Such a system scarcely put membership in the Farm Bureau on a voluntary basis, particularly when all credit for securing the benefit payment checks was attributed to Farm Bureau efforts in Washington. A recent directive from the Secretary of Agriculture has instructed the several state extension services to separate themselves from sponsorship or financial support by any private organization.

The National Agricultural Workers Union

The National Agricultural Workers Union in no sense represents a movement among farmers comparable to those we have already discussed. It calls for attention here only because it represents a type of movement which, with the rise of tenancy and migrancy, may become characteristic of rural life. Grange, Farmers' Union, and Farm Bureau, we have seen, are concerned to see that the farmer secures a greater share of the total national income. At least in theory they band all farmers together to secure a more adequate return on their effort through cooperative buying and selling, through better and more efficient production methods, through crop control and marketing agreements, and through political action on state and federal governments. The National Agricultural Workers Union, on the other hand, is not concerned to band all farmers together but rather to secure a greater proportion of the total income available to agriculture for a certain group of farmers, specifically small owner-operators, tenants, and day laborers. This is such a new departure as to require our consideration, even though the movement itself is of small proportions and meager influence.

Something of the plight of tenants in the cotton South has already been indicated in the chapters dealing with the land. Most of these tenants are on farms too small for a balanced agriculture. They are engaged in a one-crop system of farming and so are dependent for livelihood on the price of cotton set on a world market, dependent on their landlords for funds to tide them over for food and clothing until the crop is harvested, and at the mercy of those landlords in any accounting of the crop. They move often, in the hope of finding richer fields, a kindlier landlord, a better house, or just change and excitement as a relief from the boredom of tenant life. When cotton prices are high and they secure a little surplus, so inured are they to poor housing and a low plane of living that the money is almost sure to be squandered through lack of knowledge of the ways and means of making daily life more comfortable in any real way.

The National Agricultural Workers Union began as the Southern Tenant Farmers Union, organized by H. L. Mitchell, a dry cleaner, and Clay East, a filling-station operator, at Tyronza, Arkansas, July 26, 1934. It is a commentary on the cultural poverty of the cotton cropper that farmers, white and Negro, came to these townsmen for help in starting a farm-tenant organization. The farmers appealed to these two men because they were socialists with a reputation for concern about underprivileged persons. They stipulated that, whatever else might be done, the organization include both white and Negro in a single membership to avoid the difficulties which had overtaken previous tenant movements divided and conquered by the race issue. General cause of the movement was the universal depression with widespread unemployment in northern cities, so that the southern agricultural malcontent had no place to go. Specific cause for organization was the fact that tenants were being mulcted by their landlords of all benefits from the developing AAA program of the federal government.

By January, 1937, the S.T.F.U. had 328 locals with 30,827 members in Texas, Mississippi, Tennessee, Missouri, North Carolina, Oklahoma, and Arkansas. Over half this number were in Arkansas, where 12.4 per cent of all tenants were members of the organization. The next largest state coverage was in Oklahoma, where 6.5 per cent of tenants were members. The number of members rose to 35,684 in 1938; later years have seen a decline in membership, because of jurisdictional disputes with the C. I. O., with which the S.T.F.U. became affiliated. It is still active as the National Agricultural Workers Union but not as powerful as in 1938, because of the trek of southern tenants to industrial jobs, the general prosperity of our cotton economy, and the interunion disputes mentioned above. Its program has been particularly effective at the following points:

1. It has defended the civil liberties of its members and established their right to organize.
2. It has secured for tenants in general full payments due on benefit awards for conformity to the cotton-acreage-reduction program.
3. It has led day laborers in strikes for higher wages and has agitated nationally for better living and working conditions for tenants and laborers.

The best indication of its effectiveness is the strenuousness of the attacks and criticism leveled at it by the southern planters, individually and as a group.

In its long-term policies the S.T.F.U. looked not to individualistic farm ownership and operation as the ideal for the working farm family but to co-operative tillage of large units with mechanical farm equipment. It believed that such farming can be more efficient and provide greater earnings to the individual farm family. It advocated a village-type economy with ownership of land vested in the individual but co-operative operation, supplemented by small industries to employ farm labor during off seasons.

It opposed crop curtailments in the light of the poverty of its own membership and urged full production together with such improvements in our system of distribution as will make the increased production available to all persons, including all types of farm labor. In contrast to other farm movements, the S.T.F.U. has:

1. Escaped the domination of the large landowners and the philosophy of individualism.
2. United white and Negro farm laborers in an organization to advance their common interests.
3. Developed a close working relationship with organized labor, with the view that the trade-union movement offers greater hope for a solution to the problems of its membership than any farmers' organization.
4. Accepted the ideal of co-operative farm operation as its long-term policy.
5. Recognized the conflict between the large-farm operator and the farm laborer and advocated collective bargaining in agriculture as a means of improving living standards.
6. Accepted a progressive point of view in regard to the necessity of fundamental changes in economic institutions.

This movement is of particular interest to churchmen, not only because it presents a new pattern in rural organization, a pattern which may have increasing utilization with increases in farm tenancy and migrancy, but also because it has had among its leaders from the very first a large number of clergymen and has phrased its appeal and program in scriptural language. In its slogans, its songs, its appeals, the S.T.F.U. has been a kind of collective Moses seeking to lead sharecroppers and day laborers in the cotton fields into a promised land of plenty. Its policies and programs have been as often defended on scriptural as on economic grounds, in ways reminiscent of the leadership of the Wesleyan local preachers in the labor movement of England and Wales during the last century. Whether for good or for ill, here religion and the church are writ large on the face of a movement for the benefit of a large segment of rural society.

In December, 1945, the name of the Southern Tenant Farmers Union was changed to "The National Farm Labor Union." More recently the name has become "National Agricultural Workers Union." The Union is now affiliated with the American Federation of Labor. A report in May, 1954, indicates that the Union has about fifty thousand members concentrated in California, Louisiana, Arkansas, and Alabama. Substantial memberships of small dairy farmers exist also in Minnesota, Wisconsin, Pennsylvania, West Virginia, and Maryland. The report concludes: "Due to poverty and the constant shifting about looking for work, especially the migrant workers, the average paid membership for the past year [1953-54] has been about 85 hundred."

The United Mine Workers

Thus far we have been discussing farmer movements, but to limit our discussion to such movements alone would be to misrepresent the organized forces at work in the rural community. Organized labor is well represented there, although the urban nature of much of our great industry leads us, all too often, to the conclusion that organized labor is an urban phenomenon. It is obviously impossible to discuss all the unions represented in rural life, but one is quite clearly a dominantly rural affair. It is no accident that the United Mine Workers is organizing dairy farmers in its District 50. Mine workers do not live in the city; they live in the isolation and privation of the mining camp, and their proximity to the farmer in daily life makes it natural for their organization to be concerned about the farmers' welfare. I do not purpose here either to defend or to attack the rightness of Mr. Lewis' policy in attempting as a labor leader to organize farmers, but to insist that miners and farmers as rural persons have a great deal in common.

The United Mine Workers of America was organized on January 23, 1890, as a merger of the Knights of Labor and the

101

Lincoln Christian College

National Progressive Union of Miners and Mine Laborers. The organization is divided roughly on geographical lines into a series of districts, and these districts control affairs within their own jurisdictions with a good deal of freedom. District 50 deserves special attention, as it is a convenient catchall into which all sorts of special organizations can be thrown. It is within District 50, for example, that the United Dairy Farmers have their existence. Since the coal miners claim jurisdiction over all unorganized workers engaged in processing coal by-products, it is easy to see that District 50 includes a miscellaneous collection of processors. Dairy farmers are included because casein from milk is used in industrial processes in combination with coal by-products.

Because coal deposits are widely scattered, miners must live in isolated mining villages to be near their work, and it was easy in earlier days to break union efforts at improvement of pay and hours by dividing one group of miners and their claims from another group. Through sad experience miners have learned that their only safety lies in joint action and complete discipline. One of their axioms of common action is that there shall be no work performed without a union contract. When a contract expires, miners regularly lay down their tools and refuse all work until the old contract is renewed or a new one drawn. More than fifty years of history stand behind this settled policy and account for the unanimity with which miners follow the dictates of their national headquarters, despite pressure from an unfriendly press and the national government. Miners trust one another and know that their strength as individuals lies directly in their working as a united group.

Something like 600,000 miners are organized in local unions, which means that the U.M.W. speaks for some two to three million people. The miners have always been concerned in the organization of other workers, first in establishing the C.I.O. to seek industrial rather than craft unionization, and now in their own programs, since the break with the C.I.O., through District 50 of the U.M.W. Some interpret this activity as representing the

102

dictatorial ambitions of one man, John L. Lewis. Others see in it the consciousness of mine workers that coal is intimately tied up with the industrial fate of the whole nation and that coal workers can prosper only as workers in related industries are able to present their point of view with vigor and organized strength. At least the pastor will find among U.M.W. members an interest that reaches far beyond the narrow horizon of the mine village and sees the welfare of people everywhere as inextricably interwoven and united.

This discussion is not a complete treatment either of the organizations mentioned or of similar organizations at work in the rural community. To make a complete analysis would require a volume in itself. The purpose has been to sense the efforts that men have made organizationally to deal with the problems of land as space, wealth, and property. The pastor will now see in these and other similar organizations something more vital than another group carrying out a social program in the community. However he may evaluate their concrete proposals, he must sympathize with their desire and purpose to bring the consolidated efforts of the community to bear on the problem of conserving our basic resources.

8

RURAL TRADE

THE HISTORY of rural America might well be written in terms of the rise and increasing importance of the trading village. The first rural Americans were subsistence farmers: they farmed not to produce a crop for the market but to supply food, clothing, and shelter for themselves and their families. In the early nineteenth century it required nine farm families to feed one city family. The farmer aimed first at supplying his own necessities and then at selling whatever was left for cash or using it in exchange for the few staple commodities he could not produce. Under such an economy the need for trading centers was relatively limited. Peddlers could meet most of the needs of the farm families, supplemented by the services of an occasional crossroads store and tavern. Even in the plantation South self-sufficiency was an ideal, for planters attempted to raise on their acres the staples to meet their own needs and those of their slaves.

Three factors working together reversed this subsistence trend in early American agriculture and made for the highly commercial agriculture of today. Settlement about the time of the War Between the States moved out onto the western plains, which are basically suited to specialized crops and large operation rather than to the general agriculture of the subsistence farmer. At about the same time the railroads came with transportation of the bulkier farm commodities at relatively low rates to the populous East and thence to the cities of Europe—cheap transportation made commercial agriculture possible. Finally the growth of American cities provided an increasing market for food staples, and the demand called for such a supply as only commercial farming methods could produce. These three forces working in conjunction brought about such a rapid commercialization of American agriculture that by 1920 one farm family was supporting itself and four other families, at the same time providing a surplus for export.

The man-power problems of the World War II period, the increased income of farmers which permitted the purchase of machinery, and the enlarging acreages that made machinery more useful have all intensified the mechanization and commercialization of agriculture, and have resulted in greater interdependence of town and country. In 1920 there were 26,500,000 horses and mules on American farms; in 1950 that number had declined to a little less than 8,000,000. In 1920 there were only 246,000 tractors on our farms; but in 1950 we had over 3,500,000 tractors. Milking machines had increased in the thirty-year period from 55,000 to 637,000; combines from 4,000 to 714,000; corn pickers from 10,000 to 456,000. And the great bulk of these increases occurred between 1940 and 1950. The American farmer came out of the Second World War with a dependence upon mechanization and commercialization which tied him for good or ill to the general commercial life of the nation and the world. For most farmers, the old semisubsistence type of independent agriculture is gone forever.

As the farm family turned increasingly to the production of cash crops for the market, it also became more and more dependent upon the market for the supply of its own immediate needs and for the handling of its products on the way to the distant consumer. The place where farm products were assembled and shipped and where farm needs were supplied became the small trading village. At intervals along the railroad there arose grain elevators, yards and chutes for the shipment of stock, lumber and coal yards, blacksmith shops, farm-machinery stores, banks, retail stores, all clustered together with the residences of their operators in little towns. The growth of the rural trading center became the mark of the developing interdependence of our rural people and the cities around the world. The mechanization of agriculture with tractors and power tools has carried further the trend to dependence upon the small town, in this case for the service, parts, and fuel which keep tractors running.

Thus trade has been historically, and is today, an important integrator of rural interests in the town-country community. We shall see that educationl, fraternal, and religious bonds pull town and country together, but it is probably true that the original and the continued basis of their unity is the mutual economic service which trade implies. The town-country community began when a village arose to be a service center, and the services which the village first provided and must still provide are economic services. Indeed, these economic services at their best contain within themselves a spiritual element which the church must sense, appreciate, and conserve.

Trade as personal

A most important characteristic of the relationship of the rural tradesman to his customer is its personal nature. One of the distinguishing marks of rural social intercourse is the sympathetic contact. The storekeeper is first a man, a neighbor, a friend, and then a tradesman. Other than cash considerations always enter into the buying or selling behavior of rural people. A bargain is never a bargain on cash terms alone, for the character and reputation of both buyer and seller always enter into the transaction. Rural people in making their purchases feel that they are investing their money not only to secure some particular satisfaction but also to help in maintaining one of the families which constitute the personal wealth of the community.

And this sense of mutual responsibility, which sometimes causes the consumer to trade to his own personal disadvantage at the store of an established neighbor, also conditions the conduct of the tradesman. For him hours of business and the letter of the contract are not particularly important considerations. He knows that his customers want his personal interest. A successful machinery salesman does not limit the maintenance service he offers to the minimum the contract provides or the hours of the normal business day. In the busy farm season he knows that a breakdown in machinery is costly to the farmer, and he plans to offer a twenty-four-hour service for repairs at such times. His concern is that his tractor should prove sufficient to the particular burden which the owner places upon it, and he expects to make the tractor go and to keep it going even at considerable cost to himself. This element of unusual and beyond-the-contract service always characterizes the conduct of really effective rural businessmen.

The small-town tradesman as scapegoat

The fact that trade is personal among rural people has also its potentialities for misunderstanding and conflict. The small-town merchant tends to become in the mind of the rural citizen the symbol of the economic system in its total aspect. When a depression comes and with it declining prices for farm products, the ordinary farmer is apt to vent his particular dissatisfactions upon the local merchant. The impersonal elements of supply and demand in a total world society are vague and unreal to him; but the merchant who pays him so small a price for his eggs, the banker who goes on collecting 5 per cent on the mortgage contracted in boom days, the elevator man who ships his wheat and returns to him so miserable a check—these are the concrete symbols of his felt misfortune. He cannot do anything about supply and demand, but he can vent his scorn and resentment on these local persons, and this he often does. The banker, who may be struggling with equal difficulty to keep his bank solvent and the funds of his depositors safe, finds himself criticized publicly, perhaps even snubbed. Knowing his own innocence and suffering in a situation which he cannot remedy, he is apt to turn bitter and show resentment against his critics.

Thus a rift develops again and again in community life because the economic misfortunes which arise from impersonal elements in the economic order are laid at the door of the small-town tradesman by his customers. Trade which brings rural persons together may also become the means of their estrangement.

The unfortunate results of this tendency to assess personal guilt for economic depressions against the local agents of the economic system are not limited to community estrangement and conflict. Equally significant is the fact that such laying of blame at the door of local tradesmen blinds rural consumers to the real cause of their distress. The economic naïveté of the average farmer and his willingness to be misled by the vendors of economic nostrums are due to the short-circuiting of his resentment to the small-town businessman. As long as he can conveniently lay the blame for his distress upon someone whom he knows and see his misfortune as the result of the other's evil designs, just so long will he neglect that intelligent participation in public affairs and that vigorous questing after real causes and remedies which are essential to economic recovery. Tradesmen and consumers have everything to gain in coming together and seeking a common solution to their common plight.

Co-operative trade

In the rural trade center an emerging influence of power and magnitude is that of the co-operative. Co-operative buying and selling are particularly congenial to rural people because of their background of mutual aid in the neighborhood. Organized co-operatives have offered to farmers in particular a systematic and large-scale method of controlling the marketing of their products and the prices of their purchases. The Grange made one of its strongest and earliest appeals, we have seen, in offering to farmers a means for acting together as producers and consumers. Many of its early efforts failed because of ignorance of the risks and pitfalls of business activity and because of lack of a systematic, well-thought-out plan for working together. Such a plan was provided in the Rochdale principles for co-operation, and these principles rest at the basis of successful co-operatives throughout rural America.

The name "Rochdale" derives from the city of Rochdale, England, where a small group of impoverished weavers set up a retail co-operative store on December 21, 1844. Their enterprise was established only after a year of saving to raise the necessary capital and of study to determine how best to organize and govern such a venture. From their study they arrived at a series of principles which they proceeded to test in practice. These principles, now generally recognized as basic to all successful co-operative businesses, include:

1. Open membership, with no discrimination in terms of religion, race, or nationality.
2. Democratic control, with voting on the basis of one vote per member regardless of number of shares held.
3. A return on invested capital limited to interest at the minimum current rate.
4. Profits of the business returned to its members in direct ratio to their patronage.

Most co-operatives also insist on doing business on a cash basis, holding aside a certain proportion of funds for co-operative education, and maintaining prices on the level of other businesses engaged in the same line of trade in the same or nearby communities. The four principles outlined above, however, constitute the foundation of successful co-operative efforts.

These principles may be applied to widely varying types of economic activity. The Rochdale pioneers began with consumer co-operation, but their early enterprise soon ramified into allied forms. At whatever point in the system of interlocking services which makes up our interdependent economic order one begins to organize co-operatively, the co-operative way moves throughout the system from this starting point with a certain inevitability. A retail grocery begins as a buying club but finds immediately that before it can sell goods, it must purchase them from a wholesale dealer. It is natural that the one retail grocery co-operative should begin to look for others with which it can organize a wholesale co-operative. When this step is taken and the wholesale co-operative enters the markets to purchase in quantity for its retail members, it soon becomes apparent that prices on certain commodities are artificially maintained at an exorbitant level. Co-operators then turn to a production co-operative in order that they may have some yardstick to judge competitive costs. Commodities as diverse as light bulbs in Sweden and fertilizer in the United States have been produced co-operatively with most salutary reductions in price on the general market as a result.

In the case of certain commodities co-operative control now functions from the taking of the raw material to the utilization of the finished product. Oil is a case in point. Co-operative oil companies now own their own wells, refineries, distribution systems, and retail outlets. Perhaps it would be more accurate to reverse the order and to indicate that the ownership of the entire enterprise rests fundamentally with the retail outlets owned by the ultimate consumer. These retail outlets, banded together co-operatively, own the other facilities for the production and distribution of oil products. Most retail co-operatives are tied in with others, at least through their membership in and ownership of a common wholesale store.

The fact that co-operative enterprises develop into larger and larger integrations should not blind us to the fact that the co-operative is basically a simple device through which ordinary people can help themselves. So it began, and so it continues to-day. Co-operatives still are born in small study groups or in a few families which begin buying together a few basic commodities. Producer co-operatives are begun when neighboring farmers band together to purchase a piece of farm machinery too costly for any one farmer to secure. The Farm Security Administration has assisted in the founding of some seventeen thousand such small-farm co-operatives. Miners, farmers, and fishermen in the isolated areas of Nova Scotia have developed co-operatives of many kinds in answer to their own basic needs under the leadership of the extension division of St. Francis Xavier University of Antigonish. Students, faced with the high rent and board charges of a university town, find that co-operative housing and eating clubs provide at once economical accommodations and happy living associations.

Within the United States co-operative techniques have now been applied on a large scale to the marketing of agricultural products, the provision of credit, the underwriting of insurance, the manufacture and distribution of electric power, oil refining and retailing, the securing of medical and hospital services, as well as the sale of farm supplies, groceries, dairy products, meat, and other consumer goods. The great bulk of this activity has developed among rural people as a result of their attempt to decide and control their economic fate. Some of it has been assisted by the federal or state governments through such agencies as the Farm Security Administration and the Rural Electrification Administration; much of it has grown up because of the activity of rural occupational organizations; a significant part of it has developed out of the activities of a few individuals in a rural community seeking a way out of their own difficulties.

Co-operatives and conflict

Co-operatives have not always, in spite of their name, promoted co-operation within the rural community. They represent a potential source of conflict, and the reasons for this ought to be clear to the rural pastor. One serious source of friction and misunderstanding is the lack of familiarity of farmers with the problems and procedures involved in storekeeping. Managing any such enterprise looks to the uninitiated outsider like an extremely simple matter; indeed, all of us are tempted to think, "Why, I could do that." The complexities of pricing, maintaining an effective inventory, keeping stocks fresh, and disposing of items that threaten to become unsalable do not appear to the surface observer. Hence the ordinary board of directors of such a concern is apt to feel that a salary high enough to command trained and experienced managership is higher than is necessary. Instead, directors employ some local person willing to enter this new field at a most modest salary and expecting to learn how to operate the establishment by operating it. It is possible that an already successful business venture could stand a little bit of such treatment, but the ordinary new and doubtful enterprise simply cannot. Ineptness in service and the failure of promised savings to materialize alienate the supporting constituency, and the venture fails. Such a failure discredits the organizers of the project and develops community rifts which endure for a generation. Particularly is this the case when the organizers give the managership to a son of one of the members or where there is any suspicion that dishonesty enters into the failure of the business.

Fully as serious as the immediate dissension in the community, however, is the reflection cast upon the co-operative enterprise in general when a local co-operative fails. Local people become increasingly skeptical about the possibility of working together and begin to entertain doubts as to the inherent capacity of ordinary men to help themselves. Such skepticism cuts, of course, at the basic faith in the ordinary man which is common to Christianity and to democracy. The failure of a co-operative involves a weakening of belief in the trustworthiness and ultimate redeemability of human nature. Such a weakening attacks the citadel of the religious life. The pastor cannot serve his community more effectively in this regard than by urging co-operative leaders to secure the best managerial services to be had when they open a co-operative. A good idea deserves the best chance of success. A letter of inquiry to the Co-operative League of the U. S. A., 343 South Dearborn Street, Chicago 4, Illinois, will bring information as to individuals trained in co-operative schools who are not only willing but prepared to accept employment and to provide a vigorous and informed leadership.

A second source of friction lies in failure properly to educate the members of a co-operative to the importance of disciplined support of their joint endeavor. Many co-operatives have been faced, when they began business, with a ruinous cut-price opposition from private establishments represented in the community. Large chain undertakings often undersell or overbid the co-operative in its infancy with the hope that such a policy will eliminate the co-operative yardstick from their trade area. Such selling or buying at a loss can be of only a relatively short duration, but the resources of the chain are economically stronger than those of the co-operative. Under such circumstances the farmer or townsman is tempted to sell to or buy from the competitor and not the co-operative. The only resource with which the co-operative can meet such treatment is the previously secured loyalty of its own members, who have been made to understand the necessity of supporting the co-operative even though prices may temporarily be better elsewhere. Wherever co-operatives have thus informed their members, the loyalty of the membership has carried them through; but many have failed because they talked easy profits and low prices without mentioning co-operative discipline. When a co-operative fails because of lack of member support, directors resent the disloyalty of their members, and the members place the burden of failure on the directors, thus fomenting community strife.

There is always the danger of strife between the organizers of a co-operative and the private tradesmen of the community, and it is probable that such strife cannot be entirely averted. Co-operators, however, can take certain precautions to see that they do as little as possible to create unnecessary misunderstanding. A price policy which does not undercut the pricing practices of the community is a beginning in the right direction. In organizing a co-operative there should be an avoidance of all misrepresentation of merchants in the community. Even where merchants are obviously unfair, it is better to appeal on the merits of co-operation and not on the demerits of private competitors. Finally, the co-operative and its members should take into account the real community service of a public-spirited private tradesman. Co-operators who trade for cash in their own store but use private facilities when they want credit are not strengthening the influence of co-operatives. A co-operative store that gratuitously adds to its services those which already are being well supplied by a local tradesman is doing itself a distinct disservice. Frictions and misunderstandings will arise, but co-operators do not need to create them.

In this chapter our focus has been upon trade as a social unifier and a social divider rather than upon trade as a purely economic activity. Among rural people the cash relationship is everywhere and always conditioned by other, more basic and emotionally conditioned relationships. Failure to appreciate this fact involves the tradesman himself in contradictions and leads the social servant, such as the minister or the teacher, to make an invalid assessment of the social relationships within the community. With trade in its purely economic aspects the minister in most cases is unqualified to deal. But no minister can afford to forget that trade has other aspects which affect and condition the personal and emotional life of the community. In these aspects he and the tradesman serve on a common front.

9

THE RURAL SCHOOL

No AGENCY is more universally present in rural life or more influential in rural society than the school. The ideal of free public education caught and held the minds of our forefathers, and they succeeded in realizing their ideal in memorable fashion. It has become fashionable in our day to raise questions as to the validity of the ideal. Certainly not all the enlightening influences which its founders anticipated as flowing from such education have been realized; but, whatever the extent of its validity, the existence and dominance of the ideal have covered the countryside with school buildings in which for a large part of five days a week for at least two thirds of the year an influential relationship exists between teachers and the youth of our society.

To begin with, it is important for the pastor to see that, no matter what the effectiveness of the teaching program in terms of its stated aims, the school is always teaching students something. It is never correct to say of a teacher, "She doesn't teach the children anything." It may be correct to say, "She doesn't teach the children what we expect them to learn." That is an entirely different matter. The contact of teacher and children for six or more hours a day, five days a week, through two thirds of the year, is bound to set its marks upon the children. They may not learn arithmetic or spelling or reading; they may learn that education is trivial, that so-called educated people are ineffectual and petty, that dishonesty pays dividends in grades and honors, that insincerity and pretense are the way to prestige and position. If they do not learn well the lessons we have set for them, they are almost sure to learn the other lessons I have listed here.

This whole matter is of concern to every citizen of the rural community, but it is of special concern to the Christian pastor, because of the dependence of the church upon the school in the development of personality. If the school has not done a comprehensive and effective job of integrating the personality of the child in the life of the wider community, then the church is under a permanent handicap as it strives to integrate the child in the life of the widest of all communities—the kingdom of God. It is perfectly possible for the school to stand directly in the way of the work of the church, not by teaching irreligion or atheism, but by encouraging the development of personalities which are one-sided and crippled in their relationship to the total community. The pastor need not be greatly concerned to have the school teach religion as such; he must insist that the school carry on its own proper work in order that he may build upon sound foundations.

Tensions in education

We can see the issues at stake more adequately if we approach the rural school and its problems in the light of certain tensions in the rural community. First is the tension between the view of education as direct participation in culture and the view of education as formal learning of the techniques of civilization. The farmer, the miner, the small townsman in general, are accustomed to learning in action. Most farm boys, for example, learn how to milk, to drive the tractor, to harness the team, and to care for machinery, not by formal training, but by participating in such activities with their fathers. They learn by acting on the spot in connection with a particular problem. Education is participation. It is natural, therefore, for the farmer to be skeptical about "book learning," to feel that time spent in classrooms under a teacher who perhaps has never milked a cow is largely wasted. However, this secondary and derived type of learning is precisely the kind of learning which is becoming more and more essential in a world in which we are increasingly dependent upon persons and forces we never see. Modern society with its interdependences must be known, if at all, through the abstractions of formal education. This does not mean that the educator cannot or will not use concrete situations in his educational method. It does mean that there is so much to learn, now that our environment is the whole world, that personal experience must be supplemented by the summary or secondhand acquaintance with facts, relationships, and methods which formal education brings.

A second tension lies in the field of school consolidation. There is, of course, no debate as to the importance of consolidation on the high-school level. A high school with a meager fifty or sixty pupils cannot afford to offer the kind of education, judged either by efficiency or by comprehensiveness, to which children today are entitled. Boys and girls from such a school who in their young maturity will come into competition with urban youth from well-equipped and splendidly taught high schools are simply not getting a fair chance from their high-school training. Whether in industry or in the college classroom, they start under a socially induced handicap. But consolidation on the primary-school level does present us with a tension between technical efficiency on the one hand and relevance to the immediate social group and its life on the other. The one-room district school is a cumbersome and costly device with a high cost per pupil and an excessive burden on the teacher. On the other hand, it is close to the homes of its pupils; its teacher may know their parents intimately; teaching becomes a less formal and a more human and understanding process. All of this *may* be, of course; there is no guarantee that it *will* be. All of us are acquainted with one-room schools which are the very antithesis of this description. If the potentialities of a one-room school are to be realized, the quality of the teacher and his training must be superior. And certainly if the one-room primary school is to be maintained, it must find its setting as a part of a larger school system to which its teacher is related for supervision and in which its pupils continue their schooling.

A third tension is that between educational need and economic resources. In 1950 the United States Census showed that 64 per cent of Americans were urban. But only 57.8 per cent of children under fifteen were urban. With only 36 per cent of Americans rural in that year, 42.2 per cent of children under fifteen were rural. These percentages mean that rural America has more than its proportion of the children of our nation to educate. Since public education is supported from local taxation, and since taxable wealth tends to pile up in cities, it should be clear that rural people with more children and less wealth have a real economic problem in providing equal educational opportunity. When we add to this the fact that the children are scattered over wide areas of countryside, so that they must be handled in small groups or transported to schools at additional cost to the taxpayer, it will be readily admitted that some kind of equalization of the educational burden between city and country is due. Since at least half of rural youth must go ultimately to the city, it is perfectly fair that the wealth of the city, to which they will ultimately contribute, should be taxed for their education. On the other hand, a difficulty arises at the point of school control. How can outside sources be tapped for the support of local schools while at the same time those schools remain the institutions and agencies of local people? The danger is that with the receipt of aid from outside the community there will come a loss of community control.

The pastor must be aware of these tensions and must help his people to be aware of them. Only as he and they realize dangers in the school situation will they be able to have a school system which reflects adequately their standards and points of view. Any educational policy or program for a community which does not come to grips with these three tensions is completely unrealistic and will, in the long run, face the community with more problems. All these tensions have origins outside the particular community and will not—cannot—be resolved by the community alone. But the community has its contribution to offer in their solution, and it must therefore take them into account. The ultimate answer to our problems lies in the experience of thousands of communities seeking humanly equitable accommodations to these dilemmas.

The indispensable teacher

All these tensions come to their ultimate practical expression in the teacher in the rural community. The one indispensable factor in a good system of education is the teacher. Good teachers will make good schools under even the most trying of material circumstances. On the other hand, even the best equipment is unproductive of educationally good results if used by a poor teacher. Any real improvement in rural education depends upon getting and keeping a high quality of teacher in the rural school; such a teacher ought to have and deserves to have the best organization and helps available, but the teacher is the prime prerequisite.

In general, rural communities have not been able, for a variety of reasons, to secure the best teachers. A most apparent factor is the low salary scale on which rural teachers are paid. To begin with, all public-school teachers receive a relatively low salary. Hutchins and Munse report in *Expenditures for Education at the Mid-Century* that in the 1949-50 school year one fourth of all teachers earned less than $2,137, one half less than $3,010, and only 10 per cent as much as $4,500. Rose Marie Smith in *Education in Rural and City School Systems* gives the data in Table VIII on page 120.

The increase which the table shows is more apparent than real, since the period covered by the data was a period of marked inflation. What the figures do show is not only the relatively disadvantaged position of the rural teacher but also the marked fluctuation in salaries of all teachers. We have certainly as a nation done little financially to indicate to our public-school teachers how vital and important we regard their work to be. We should not be surprised if industry continually attracts able teachers away from the schoolroom.

TABLE VIII

Comparative Average Annual Salaries for Rural and
Urban School Teachers for Selected Dates

	1935-36	1941-42	1947-48
Rural Teachers	$ 844	$1,009	$2,086
Urban Teachers	1,874	2,072	3,174

These figures, however, do not indicate the inadequate standard of living available to the average rural teacher. It is not unusual for such a person to be unable to find any satisfactory place within the community to live. Sometimes he, or she, is given board and room by turns in the homes of a farming neighborhood, spending a week in each home. Such arrangements, of course, provide little, if any, privacy for study and preparation, and no opportunity for the development of living quarters expressive of the tastes and preferences of the teacher himself. Even when good physical accommodations are available at a reasonable figure, the society of other persons of similar ages and tastes is almost always lacking. Company for the necessary moments of relaxation just does not exist in many rural communities, from which youth of the teacher's age and interests have gone to the city.

A third reason for the failure of rural communities to command the services and loyalty of the better teachers lies in the attitude of suspicion with which the teacher is treated by many school boards. Teachers are surrounded by all sorts of restrictive rules: they are to remain in the community over the week end two weeks out of every month; women teachers are not to have dates with local young men; no teacher is to have a date on any school night; teachers are not permitted to smoke—we might extend the list indefinitely. All these rules have, we hope, the best possible motives behind them. They seek to provide morally excellent and community-concerned leadership for youth in school. But morality and devotion to the community are free achievements of the person; they cannot be compelled. When the school-board chairman, with a cigar draped from the corner of his mouth, demands that a young man sign a contract in which he promises not to smoke, we can scarcely expect the young man to avoid making the inference that he is regarded as an immature inferior. A person of spirit, such as we hope our teachers will be, should throw such a contract in the waste-basket and leave the board to its own devices. And better teachers—while they may not throw contracts into the waste-basket—leave communities where they are so treated.

A recent study by the National Education Association (Research Bulletin, Volume XXI, Number 1) indicates that rural teachers do not feel under pressure in these matters as they once did. But a new type of pressure is now being felt. Teachers feel that there are certain subjects which they must steer around in their teaching. Sex, socialism, communism, the current political scene, are all viewed as matters wisely ignored in the classroom. Rural Americans must decide whether or not they wish their children to grow up believing that these important matters are not subject to rational interpretation and evaluation. Teachers who in their own insecurity reflect the fears of their fellow citizens are not adequate mentors for a coming generation of free men and women.

Behind such treatment lies an extremely low estimate of education and a consequent low valuation of the lives of our children. The Christian pastor should sense this fact and make it explicit to his people that the schoolteacher is, in actuality, one of the chief influences for good or ill in the community.

Every effort should be made to secure teachers who are colorful and intelligent personalities, and they should be given the freest possible hand in their guidance of youth, their only restriction being a sense of the trust which the community reposes in them.

The church serving teachers

We have already indicated the vital stake which the pastor has in the welfare of the schools. What is his particular function in this connection? First of all, to be the friend and community champion of the schoolteachers. Let them find in him one person who treats them as human beings, important and wanted in their own right. In entering a new community the pastor should become acquainted as soon as possible with the superintendent of schools, the principals of the schools, and, insofar as it is practicable, with the individual teachers. Where there are district schools in the open country, he ought to introduce himself to the teacher when he is first near a particular school and make it a practice to stop at the school for a visit whenever he is engaged in routine calling in the vicinity. Such a call should be informal, and he should not come with a ready lecture on tap to give to the pupils. His concern should be rather to understand what the school is doing, to sense some of the problems the teacher faces, and to express appreciation of good work being done. Particularly when a new and untried teacher is beginning work in a one-room school, it is important to visit early in the fall. Relatively simple problems of discipline may then be developing which later, if unchecked, may hurt the teacher's effectiveness. The sense of support he or she may secure from the pastor's visit, the encouragement the pastor can give, and the adjustments that are achieved through a quiet word to parents or individual pupils may make all the difference between success in a first school and disheartening failure.

Many communities now hold a reception for the teachers in the autumn when school begins. Such a reception is most appropriately sponsored by the churches of the community. Where there is only a single church, the necessary planning is obviously easy. Where there are several churches, the ministers may well come together at the call of one of their number to discuss the feasibility of a special social occasion, and then constitute a committee from the several church constituencies. The reception might be held in the church parish hall, where a single church is involved, or in some community center if more than one church is concerned. But whatever the specific arrangements, the emphasis should be always upon the importance of the work of the teacher for the whole community and the trust which the community reposes in him.

Where living quarters are a problem, the pastor again may be of help to teachers. Occasionally he is able to make room for them in his own parsonage, and this is a service deeply appreciated in a community where his is generally among the best homes. Often he is able to persuade some of the more comfortably housed families in the community to make a spare room available to a teacher. When these courses are impossible, he may well take steps toward the provision of a "teacherage" for the use and comfort of the younger or unmarried teachers. It is distinctly worth the investment of money on the part of the community as a whole to provide living quarters so cheerful and comfortable that the teachers will naturally remain in the community over week ends. To urge a teacher, or to require him, to remain through a long week end in dreary, cold, uncomfortable quarters is to assure the development in him of a sense of frustration and rebellion. Such an attitude will color his teaching and handling of pupils throughout the week. If teachers cannot have comfortable, friendly living quarters, they should be encouraged to leave town over the week end in the interest of the mental health of their charges.

Further than this, we can see to it that the new teacher is given a place in the social life of our people. An invitation to a Saturday's hunting or fishing with the pastor and a friendly layman may be all that is needed to start a young man on his proper path in community life. Friday-night dinner at the parsonage is good for both the teachers and the preacher's family. Picnics, sleigh rides, skating parties, to which the teacher is made a party, are all a source of joy not only to him but to the preacher as well. And the pastor can see to it that similar invitations are forthcoming from various families in the community. Warmth, concern, trust, on the part of local people inevitably breed similar attitudes in the teachers who come to a community.

There is always a temptation to use schoolteachers for teaching positions in the Sunday church school. This is unwise, if not positively bad, for several reasons:

1. It confronts the children with the same personality on Sunday as during the week—variety helps the educational process.
2. It provides no rest, relaxation, or contrasting activity for the teacher himself.
3. Worst of all, it keeps local people who are not teachers from learning to teach and from experiencing the joys which come in leading youth forward in Christian experience.

Many of us can recall the profound influence of some Sunday-school teacher—an influence as much dependent upon his long reputation for fair dealing in the community as upon his knowledge of and skill in teaching. Schoolteachers ought to be used instead in other positions of church leadership. They may sing in the choir, serve on boards and committees, preside as officers of the various auxiliary groups of the church. In such employment they find a needed contrast to their regular work as teachers.

So much for the integration of the teacher in the life of the community. I have treated this apparently insignificant matter at length because only teachers who feel themselves a part of the community, who sense that they are trusted and wanted as persons, can teach that love and appreciation of rural life which is the proper heritage of every country boy and girl. We have a procession of rural youth to the city in part because they follow the attitudes and ideals established in their minds by their teachers. Teachers whose experience of rural life is tinctured with pettiness, suspicion, and galling restrictions will effectually transfer their own impression to their impressionable charges. An embittered and frustrated teacher is a menace to rural values of every kind. Social breakdown within the rural community begins with the parent or teacher who cannot find root there.

Beyond all this, we must be concerned with the professional competence of the teacher himself. It is important that the community secure as well trained a teacher as is possible. Experience, unless it is professionally supervised and guided, is not a substitute for training. In general, a well-trained but inexperienced teacher is to be preferred to one with experience but inferior training—school boards to the contrary notwithstanding. Unguided and uncriticized experience often confirms one in bad teaching habits, while proper training provides one with good habits to begin with. More important than an excellent grade record for the rural teacher is an indication of imagination and originality in meeting problems. A person with fine grades may simply have an excellent memory. And since his formal training will be colored inevitably by urban standards, it may not serve the rural teacher adequately in his particular rural situation. To do a proper job, he needs the additional qualities of imagination and resourcefulness.

When such a teacher is discovered, he or she should be encouraged to go ahead experimentally with a long-term program in view. Nothing will do more to prevent the tremendous turnover in rural teachers which we now have than involving good teachers in long-range programs which they will desire to follow through on their own. Rural communities can pay better salaries than they now do, but they can never hope to compete with city school systems in monetary terms. What they can offer to excellent teachers is freedom of experiment and to grow as a wanted and important part of community life. In offering such freedom and social support to our teachers, we make possible the growth of free and mature personalities in our sons and daughters. A community's cultivation of strong and independent teaching is one of the best measures of its realistic concern for its children.

10

OTHER EDUCATIONAL AGENCIES
AND PROGRAMS

THOUGH THE bulk of work in the rural school itself is done with children and youth, the school is increasingly reaching out to co-operate in informal educational programs which affect adults as well. The Smith-Hughes vocational agriculture teacher in the high school, for instance, is paid largely by funds from the federal treasury, and is employed, not for the nine months of the school year, but for an eleven-month term. During the summer months he works with his pupils, organized in the Future Farmers of America, in supervising projects on their home farms. Thus he is in contact with the men of the community and has a very definite educational relationship to them. Enterprising high-school principals are further making school buildings available for adult groups and are even aiding in provision of educational leadership in meeting adult interests and needs.

Library service

The rural school is not the sole agency of education in rural life; rather it works with and is supplemented by other agencies and programs. Its chief educational ally is a good library. The American Library Association has stated that unfortunately only one third of our rural population has good library service, another third has library service of more or less inadequate type, but for the final third there is no library service of any description. Thus for a large proportion of rural Americans no library resources are available to supplement the training of the school and to help in understanding our rapidly changing contemporary life.

Efforts are being made on several fronts to remedy this lack. States and counties are organizing "Bookmobile" services, whereby a supply of books is taken out in a specially equipped trailer or truck to isolated districts, there to be loaned to the local people. State libraries increasingly are making books available by mail. High schools are opening their libraries for general and public use. Such services can often be supplemented by the church. In one Michigan hamlet without library facilities the pastor discovered that books were available for his people from the state library at Lansing, but found himself faced with the problem of how to get the books to people for whom the correspondence required in mail borrowing was too involved. The first step in the solution of his problem came with the realization that in his own church building was a large vestibule which could be heated separately from the church proper, and which was at the time serving no particular purpose. It was an easy matter to enlist the interest of church members and constituency, and soon a full-fledged project was under way. Volunteer labor using donated lumber built shelves along the inner walls of the vestibule; interested persons donated chairs and tables for library browsing; the pastor secured a supply of books on loan to the village from the state library; and members of the women's society agreed to take charge on certain afternoons and evenings. Thus, at no great cost, good literature was made available to all the people of the community. This sort of project any church can undertake.

Where library services do exist, they are frequently lacking in religious literature, however well they may be stocked in other lines. On dusty shelves have accumulated the forbidding volumes given so lovingly by former pastors in the community. Good books in their own day, they are now outgrown but, alas, unreplaced. They effectually discourage anyone who seeks to take an intelligent interest in contemporary religious life and thought. By their presence on the shelves they create the impression that religion itself is forbidding and outworn. Here the church has the opportunity to lift the religious reading level of the whole community. When the subscriptions are sent in for the denominational paper, why not include a subscription for the library? Similarly, good religious books may well be given to the library for general circulation. Certainly every church should be concerned to see that well-bound and clearly printed copies of the various translations of the Bible are in the library.

The county agent (farm adviser)

Foremost among educational enterprises not connected with the public schools is the program of the extension service of the United States Department of Agriculture. The local representative of this program is the county agent, who is supported by local and federal funds. Sometimes, as in Illinois, his local support is raised by the Farm Bureau; sometimes, as in Wisconsin, the county pays the local expense; but the county agent's responsibility is to all the farmers of his area in either case. Support by the Farm Bureau or other private agency has recently been ruled out by a directive of the Secretary of Agriculture. The minimum staff is a county agent and his secretarial help. The agent is an individual specially trained at an agricultural college and periodically called in for refresher courses. He may have as his assistant in charge of home-economics work with farm women a woman trained likewise in the college of agriculture. If his work is very extensive, he may have a male assistant who is in charge of a section of the county under his direction; and he may have a club leader, either a man or a woman, in charge of the 4-H Club work of the county. Where he works alone, the county agent himself is responsible for all these various activities. In some states the older term "county agent" has been supplemented by the new designation "farm adviser."

The county agent works from an office, generally in the courthouse at the county seat. There he is regularly available at stated times for consultation on particular problems. A farmer may bring in a weed taken from one of his fields, a weed which he does not recognize or is not able to control. If the agent does not recognize it himself, he consults various reference books in his technical library, and perhaps he is able to give the farmer an experiment-station research bulletin telling him exactly how to combat this particular weed. If he meets difficulty in identifying the weed, he sends the sample to extension-service headquarters at the state college. There the weed is examined and identified by trained experts, and instructions are dispatched to the farmer through the agent as to how to treat it. Should the weed prove unusual for that part of the country—a new intruder—the experts may even come to the county in question, inspect the fields which are infested, and prescribe on the spot. Particularly difficult diagnoses or prescriptions are referred to the research staff of the Department of Agriculture in Washington, D. C. Thus the working farmer, through his county agent, has the resources of the state college and experiment station and the United States Department of Agriculture at his call in the problems which he finds on his own farm.

From time to time the county agent calls meetings of the farmers for purposes as varied as explaining the new income-tax rulings as applied to farm income, discussing labor pooling in relationship to farm-labor shortages, or providing the latest information on artificial insemination of dairy cows. In such matters of concrete farm practice as artificial insemination the meeting may be called at one of the farms and an actual demonstration of the technique provided. Out of such demonstrations may come plans for co-operative use of a purebred sire, with the county agent assisting the farmers to arrange the various details of such co-operative endeavor.

The above suggests how quickly the work of the county agent moves over from purely educational to action programs. During recent years county agents have organized farmers for co-operative purchase of carload lots of agricultural limestone;

they have secured TVA fertilizers for test use. They handle the importation of foreign farm laborers in farm-labor shortage areas. If new crops are to be developed in a county or new systems of tillage to be tried, the county agent often helps with the cultivation of demonstration fields on various farms scattered strategically throughout the county. Education, demonstration, and action are closely linked in the extension program.

Land-use planning

In 1938 there was inaugurated the "County Land-Use Planning" idea, which may prove to be one of the most effective democratic methods of managing the soil as a national trust. This program is largely in the hands of the county agent and generally is effectively or nominally pursued in terms of his particular interest. The plan calls for the division of a county into community areas, within each of which a mass meeting of farmers is called to discuss the advisability of developing a land-use planning program. Out of such a meeting are organized neighborhood committees and a community committee, and out of the several meetings held throughout the county a general county committee emerges. The neighborhood committees study the land in their neighborhoods—often a township is used for convenience—and develop a system of land classification. They may classify the land somewhat as follows:

1. Level land of good quality suitable for crops
2. Level land poorly drained, requiring co-operative action for drainage to make it usable
3. Rolling land beginning to erode, best put into permanent pasture
4. Hill lands to be put into permanent forest, on a farm wood-lot basis
5. Waste lands best used as public forest for recreational purposes.

Their classification is then turned over to the community committee for integration with the work of other similar committees. Last of all, the community classifications are integrated by the county committee in a unified land-use plan for the county.

How can such a plan be made to work in a nation where land is privately owned? One of the mechanisms through which this is done is the taking up of tax-delinquent lands by the appropriate governmental unit. When these lands are unsuitable for cultivation, they are returned to their appropriate use under the land-use plan. When they are suitable for crop cultivation, they are offered to farmers whose land ought to be removed from cultivation in exchange for their poorer acreages. In almost every such case the farmer in question sees the value to himself and his family of moving to better land and readily avails himself of the opportunity. Thus important and necessary land-use adjustments, impossible to the individual farmer alone, are made through organized and democratic group action.

Out of this land-use planning program have come some most amazing developments. County committees have discovered that their problem is as much one of men as of land. "Who is to operate this land tomorrow?" is the question they have found themselves asking. This question has instigated youth surveys to determine whether local youth wished to remain on the farm and whether young people had or could acquire the resources necessary for farm operation and ownership. Barron County in Wisconsin, Blackford County in Indiana, and Culpeper County in Virginia have all conducted most illuminating studies. In general they indicate that only half our farm boys and girls can remain on the farms if farms of adequate and economic size are to be available to them. Thus rural communities must prepare at least half their young people for vocational adjustment and achievement in other than farm work.

Culpeper County, Virginia, has gone a step further and studied its churches as one of the fundamental resources in any plan for people on the land. Our own discussion in earlier chapters of the dependence of the church upon land use and the responsibility of the church in proclaiming a stewardship of the land indicates how significant such a study is. As we have seen, where land is worn-out and poor, churches are economically poor; but the relationship is not necessarily a simple one of cause and effect. Perhaps "poor" churches—churches which, neglecting the discipline of stewardship, leave their members with no sense of the soil as holy, given to man by God—are the original cause of poor land. Certainly land-use planning committees should find in the Christian pastor a sympathetic ally in their attempt to plan for a permanent agriculture.

4-H Clubs

Best known of the county agent's activities is his sponsorship of 4-H Clubs. The four H's stand for Hand, Health, Head, and Heart. The clubs are small, consisting of from eight to a dozen boys and/or girls under the guidance of a local leader. Each club has a specific vocational project: it is a calf club or a sewing club or a bread-baking club. Projects cover the fields of agriculture, animal husbandry, home economics, manual arts, and sometimes even the fine arts. Each club member is required to complete a project during the club year and to exhibit it for criticism and grading by the county agent, the club agent, or some other qualified judge. Especially excellent projects are exhibited in competition for prizes at county and state fairs. In recent years an unfortunate competitive element has entered the 4-H Club movement in its national aspects through prizes and other awards offered by packing houses and the like. The offering of extrinsic awards for excellence is essentially foreign to the basic 4-H Club idea, which is fine work for its own sake.

The pastor and church leaders may well offer to sponsor 4-H Clubs in their neighborhoods or make available to already existing clubs the use of church facilities. Often local clubs within a community area will appreciate the privilege of using the church social rooms for a fair and exhibit at the close of their club year. Such a fair offers the church an opportunity to show its concern for agriculture as a way of life. It also offers to the 4-H Club movement an opportunity to make more of the Heart among the four H's than it generally is able to do.

Our review of the work of the county agent indicates the miscellaneous enterprises, educational and demonstrational, which he carries out. Not all these activities will be in the program of every county agent. Depending upon temperament, training, and experience, some agents will be more concerned about farm production problems, some more interested in marketing and management, while others will see the importance of the social problems of rural life. An effective agent, while he may have his own particular hobby, will offer to the farmers of his county a program in which all these concerns are represented. As soon as he enters a new rural parish, a pastor should learn something of the program of the county agent in his particular community.

Miscellaneous agencies

A discussion of rural education would not be complete without some mention of other educational agencies within the local community. We have already noted that farm organizations have their educational programs. On technical agricultural matters these programs are excellent; on wider social problems they tend to be one-sided and biased. In presenting the case of the commercial farmer they are apt to ignore the welfare of the consumer and the small farmer, tenant, and farm laborer, while they may misrepresent the point of view and attitude of organized labor. All farmers' co-operatives have educational programs dealing with the production and marketing of agricultural commodities, but some of the worst labor baiting in recent years has been indulged by various producing and marketing co-operatives.

Various farm-machinery companies sponsor one-day institutes and fairs, in which astute advertising of their product is mingled with advice as to new methods of tillage and labor-saving short cuts. Similarly, electric power and gas companies provide institutes in which the use of electric power or gas fuel on the farm and in the farm home is explained and recommended. While these commercial programs of education have a propaganda element and are certainly devised to benefit the company in question, they often make available to rural people ideas and techniques which make farm work easier and more effective and enrich farm home life. Anyone who has observed in the farm home the difference which the transition from lamplight to electric light can bring will understand how helpful commercial programs devised to make electricity more usable may be.

The Parent-Teacher Association is a familiar educational group in many rural communities. As a medium for the interchange of ideas and the development of a common front between the home and the school it is an invaluable activity. Locally it seeks to inform the parents as to the meaning of new school developments and to give to teachers some evaluation of their work in terms of home reactions. It often sponsors such extracurricular activities in the school as require outside financial support and thus comes to have a special vested interest in a particular activity. There is always the danger that such interest will supplant that general concern for the whole life of the pupil in home and school which is the avowed purposes of the P.T.A. It is important that this organization serve its fundamental purpose as the agency of intercommunication between parents and teachers in the problems of in-school youth.

All this listing of educational enterprises in the rural community serves but to emphasize to the rural pastor that the church in its educational work is not operating in a vacuum but is one of a series of educational agencies within its community. With all these agencies the church will find itself in common cause, insofar as all are seeking to enrich and conserve rural life. Wherever they seek to enrich rural life at the expense of other groups within our own country or around the world, or whenever they seek to set group against group within rural society itself, we must oppose them in the interest of the very people they are trying to help. This means that the educational task of the church is broader than we have been accustomed to think. Sunday school and vacation church school are not enough; for, while they affect our members for good, we must reach out to the whole community.

Press, radio, and television

One important avenue for a community-wide approach is the village or county newspaper. Such papers are always looking for news and will all publish newsworthy items which we send them. Items which deal in interesting fashion with the world missionary program of the church, with the pronouncements of church bodies on world events and the place of agriculture in world life, with rural experiments being carried on under church auspices, offer an antidote to the provincialism and particularism of all too much rural education. Reprint privileges can often be secured for excellent articles in religious journals of the denomination. Since such articles will be printed in the local newspaper only as we make it our business to get them to the editor, each rural church ought to have a wide-awake publicity committee aiming not only to present to the public the various programs of the local church but also to present to all in the community some picture of what the world church means and is doing.

Another equally important avenue of community education among rural people is the radio. Pastors generally experience it as a hindrance rather than an ally. Many farm families turn the radio on in the morning and off when they retire at night. How often our calls are a nightmare of dodging in and out among announcers and swing bands with the good news of the Kingdom. Again, the radio brings to our people the selfish appeal of the commercial evangelist and pumps local rural resources out of the community into his personal treasury in the city. An elderly woman handed the pastor, who had served in her parish for two years, a small sum of money when he called, saying: "I was starting to send this to Brother Blank (a radio evangelist), as I do regularly, when I thought: 'Perhaps our own preacher could use a little money.'" But the fact that the radio has been a handicap does not mean that we should neglect it; rather we should attempt to redeem it for the gospel's sake.

A group of families chosen by their pastors as representing the best piety of their respective churches told me of their radio listening habits. On the average fewer than one in ten of the programs they regularly listened to was religious in any sense. As a matter of fact, few of the programs had any serious purpose at all. More than a third of them were variety programs. Variety and serials together accounted for 60 per cent of the programs listed. This would not be unusual in the average family, but these were not average families; they were families with whom their professional religious leaders were most satisfied. If the radio is so little a religious influence with such families, how much less must be its religious effects upon the run-of-the-mill members of our churches!

Every pastor can be sure that his people know when the notable religious broadcasts take place on Sunday. Special mention of them should be made from time to time in our bulletins; a permanent listing of the broadcasts with time and station should be posted on the bulletin board of the church. A discussion of issues raised in specific broadcasts and reference in our sermons to particular statements are other ways of keeping the fact of these excellent radio services before our people. This is only a beginning. Wherever we can, we should make use of the radio ourselves for presenting a Christian point of view. When invitations come to preside at devotions on the small local station, they ought to be accepted, not as occasion for rehashing sermons, but as opportunity for development of a devotional program which takes advantage of the special potentialities of radio presentation.

Hitherto television has been limited in its outreach into the countryside because of the short broadcasting range of the installations and their location almost exclusively in metropolitan centers. But this is no longer the case, as witness the television aerials that plunge and teeter skyward above village and farm homes along the highways of rural America. Whether the decentralization of broadcasting facilities will lead to more local and live programs is not clear. The county ministerial association should stand ready, however, to develop and sponsor local religious telecasts, should the opportunity develop. Help in such matters is available through the radio and television committees and commissions of the several denominations, of state councils of churches, and of the National Council of Churches of Christ in the U. S. A.

At present there is no effective religious program on radio or television specifically directed to the mind of rural people. Advertisers and politicians give our people special attention, but the church has passed them by. In the near future some enterprising county ministerial association will develop a program geared to the thinking and needs of rural people. Rural pastors ought to plan and to experiment as opportunity comes to them, in order that they may use the radio with the utmost effectiveness.

In the midst of agencies and programs bombarding the community with propaganda and appeals, the church has a special function in calling to mind standards and principles by which appeals must be judged. The steady and reiterated presentation of these standards and principles to all people in our community is the only possible course open to the church in a day of crisis like our own. Our co-operation with these various educational presentations must be in terms of the defining gospel. Only thus can we serve our people in making possible an integrated and abiding community and national life.

11

RURAL WELFARE

MOST OF US have become familiar during the last twenty-five years with the word "welfare" as applied to services seeking the amelioration of the lot of underprivileged people. Into our thinking has come a conviction that the lifting of every person and family to a minimum standard of health and decency is a duty resting upon the total body politic. However we may interpret individual cases, we are now generally agreed that the assistance the government may bring to its citizens is not charity but a socially necessary ministry.

This whole concept of social welfare has a religious rootage. The first services to unfortunates began in the cities of our country through church missions and settlement houses. While the first welfare agencies were under religious auspices and all churches still maintain some such services in large urban centers, most efforts are now in the hands of private philanthropic agencies. With the almost complete breakdown of our economic arrangements in the early 1930's, the government, first state and then federal, stepped in to bring the resources of its taxing and borrowing power to bear upon a problem too gigantic for any lesser powers to master. Our thought has moved from a concept of relief as simple physical maintenance, through the concept of maintenance on a level of good health, to the present concept of maintenance as involving family and individual morale as well as physical well-being. What we have to consider here is the meaning of all this for and in the rural community.

Rural health

Health is one of the first concerns of any welfare program. Rural people have always taken their good health as a matter of course. Living in a relatively simple and healthful environment, eating a variety of fresh vegetables, plentifully supplied with milk and eggs, and engaged in work which gives exercise to all resources of the individual, both physical and mental, they have maintained a level of health and vigor markedly above that of their city cousins. Having said this, we must add that there are many areas in rural America in which living conditions are so inferior that the health conditions of the inhabitants are on a par with those of the city slum dweller. Particularly is this true in wide areas of the rural South and among Mexicans in the Southwest. The contrast between rural and urban health is now not nearly so marked as it has been in the past. Medical science has made its great contributions to public health in the cities of America. The urban death rate is still higher than the rural, but it has decreased much more rapidly. Furthermore, there is every reason to believe that this situation will continue, inasmuch as there are fewer doctors practicing in rural areas than a generation ago. Further, modern medical practice has come to depend more and more on the hospital for diagnosis and treatment, and hospitals are few among rural people.

Not only are doctors fewer in rural communities, but their charges are often heavier to rural people than they would be in the city. This is due to the fact that many doctors charge a mileage rate of fifty cents to a dollar a mile for a call at the patient's home. Obviously a farmer sixteen miles distant from the doctor's office has to be very sick before he will call the physician. We have already dealt with this and other such costs in connection with the problem of land as space. Unfortunately, by the time a man is very sick, it is often too late for the doctor to help him a great deal. Modern medical science depends upon seeing the patient early in his illness and warding off the serious effects of delay, yet the system of charges which the doctor uses makes an early call unlikely.

Many rural counties have established a public-health system, of which the visiting nurse is the symbol and representative. She is paid by county funds, sometimes assisted by state aid, and makes only a nominal charge to those able to pay for her services. She is particularly effective in prenatal, confinement, and postnatal care. Her business is to get back to the most isolated people, to discover their health needs, and to remedy them. Sometimes she works through the schools where there is no school nurse, examining children for remediable defects. Teeth, tonsils, adenoids, nutritional defects, and developmental deficiencies and anomalies are her concern among rural children.

Health is one of the chief concerns of the Christian gospel. Jesus in his ministry was never indifferent to the burdens which poor health laid upon personality. Again and again he gave his attention, not to the crowd gathered about him to hear his words, but to the individual brought to him for healing and strength. We show ourselves indifferent to health only at great peril to the total gospel message; for, when we neglect to stress health, the sectarians of every doctrine and temper come to our people with their misinterpretations of the Christian ideal. On foreign mission fields the church still maintains health services; there is no reason why the church should not become the sponsor of such services at home where they are lacking.

Churches may properly band together to establish a dispensary and to organize community support for a physician. In the community council they may suggest and support some system, either of flat charges or of equalization of health-service opportunity through the use of tax funds to make the charge for a doctor's call the same for everyone within the community area. Often the community will be too small an area for this pooling, and the county will be taken as the unit for medical service. The only way of telling how large an area must be taken as the fundamental medical-service unit is to study the particular situation, including such factors as number of people to be served, doctors available, road and weather conditions, and general economic status of the people. In appealing for life decisions for Christian service, the church ought to lay before its young people the possibility of serving as doctors and nurses in areas of particular need.

Health is more a matter of proper care all the time than one of special care in times of illness. Many rural persons, sometimes whole neighborhoods in areas of one-crop agriculture, are chronically undernourished; yet all rural people can be well fed with a little attention to balancing diets. Abundant information in this regard is now available through the extension service of the Department of Agriculture. If members of your church and community are not getting such information, then it is up to you to arrange for presentations in the women's organization or in a general community meeting. Church suppers may well serve the cause of health if those in charge make sure that the meals are properly balanced and tempting, for homemakers are quick to respond to novel or varied suggestions in menu. Wherever there is a home agent of the extension service in a county, she will be glad to work with officers and committees in arranging church-supper plans. Where there is no home agent, a letter to the state office of the extension service at the state agricultural college will bring suggested menus and perhaps indications of offices where personal guidance may be secured.

Mental health is a growing problem in rural America. Studies published since the close of World War II are disconcerting in the data they provide indicating a relatively higher incidence of mental and emotional disorders among rural draftees. And most psychiatrists and behavior clinics are in urban areas. There are, however, state institutions and clinics available to rural as well as urban people, and the pastor ought to know what resources are available to meet the needs of the mentally disturbed.

The pessimism as to the outcome of the disease with which we once greeted mental disorder is no longer justified. Each year finds more cures and better cures effected. This ministry to the troubled of mind is a primary responsibility of the rural church, a responsibility it best carries out by conference with other agencies, by co-operation in wider programs of community education, and by referral to specialized agencies and institutions.

Economic welfare: the farmer

Welfare means, however, something more than good health for all the people of our community; it means also an economic support for these people when they are unable to support themselves. Such failure in self-support may arise from a variety of causes, and each cause requires its own remedy. Sometimes there is a general failure of economic support in the community because of a natural cataclysm—fire, earthquake, flood, or drought. Such emergency need is met by the Red Cross and the various agencies of the federal government, with the Army sometimes sent in to maintain order, to prevent looting, to do necessary relief and rescue work. Food may be provided from surpluses purchased from farmers by the federal government. When a community is prostrated by a natural catastrophe, outside aid offers the only possible relief.

A second cause for an inadequate economic support is general economic depression. When the entire business order is thrown into serious deflation, farmer and nonfarmer alike are put in a serious economic plight. Let us look at the farmer's condition first. Farm production cannot be curtailed in the same way as industrial production; fields bear, cattle mature, cows give milk, without reference to business cycles. Indeed, a decline in farm prices may actually be followed by an increase in production, since the individual farmer will feel that he has to raise more to earn as much as he previously did. When farm prices decline, only farmers on the best land and with very slight overhead costs can produce at a profit. Others produce more and more at a greater and greater loss. Finally they cannot meet interest and principal payments on their mortgages and consequently lose even the right to farm at a loss. Thus, through no fault of their own, they become economically insolvent, because of the general condition of our economic life.

Americans are coming to see that personal failure resulting from general economic disorder is a public and social responsibility requiring a public remedy. They are also seeing that, where that failure is connected with so valuable a resource as land, the public remedy must be so applied as to safeguard the land as well as the individual or family on the land. Thus the Agricultural Adjustment Program was devised to give benefit payments to farmers for withholding part of their acreage from production and so preventing the accumulation of market surpluses. But these payments were given only when the farmer adopted for the land in question soil-enriching and soil-conserving practices. His welfare guaranteed by better prices was one important matter, but the welfare of the soil for future generations was equally important.

An increasingly important concept in this field is that of "parity." Farm organizations insist that price ceilings on agricultural goods should not be set below parity. Parity requires that a farmer receive for a bushel of corn today a price large enough to purchase goods and services equivalent to those he got for a bushel of corn in a base period. The base period for most commodities is 1910-14, since it is agreed that agriculture and industry were in relative balance during those years. For some commodities, for one or another special reason, another base period is used, and legislation now sets a sliding average over prior ten years in determining a base price. It is important to note that parity does not mean that corn should sell now at the average price of corn during the years 1910-14. Parity takes into account also the exchange value of the dollar, so that a farmer is to receive for his bushel of corn, not a money equivalent, but the equivalent in the things he buys and uses.

There is a crude justice in the idea of parity; after all, a man ought to receive relatively the same return for the same labor over the long span of the years. But the actual working of the parity concept must be closely watched and frequently revised in the interest of total justice. To freeze agricultural returns at the 1910-14 level is to fail to take into account advances in technology of agricultural production which have occurred since that date. Is the farmer to pre-empt all the advantages of such new departures and economies as are possible through hybrid seed corn and rubber-tired tractors? Justice requires that such socially produced technological advances and their consequent economies be shared between producer and consumer. Recent revisions of parity formulas take into account prices in more recent periods in determining the base price.

Currently there is much debate as to whether farm prices should be supported by government loans at a fixed parity ratio (90 per cent of parity is generally named), or whether the support should be on a flexible basis sinking to perhaps 75 per cent of parity with a surplus production in a particular commodity. Associated with this debate is the bold suggestion of former Secretary of Agriculture Brannan that the support of prices should be in terms of income to the farmer and that the actual market price of farm products should be allowed to seek its own level in terms of supply and demand. Such a plan would mean that the farmer would get a check directly from the government for the difference between the actual figure at which he sold his crop and the parity price. It would mean that consumers would get the advantage of good crop years in lower prices over the counter; though they would still pay, as they now do, a subsidy to the farmer through taxation. Mr. Brannan added to this a limitation of subsidy to the first 1,800 units of a farmer's production so that large commercial enterprises would not secure this subsidy on their entire crop. His argument was that what Americans wish to do is to help the family farmer and not to subsidize the large-scale corporation farm. It is this latter aspect of his plan which probably motivates much of the virulent criticism launched against it. It should be noted that in 1953 wool went under a price-support scheme very similar to the one Mr. Brannan advocated.

So much for the welfare of farmers in general. The welfare of the lowest third of the farmers is the concern of the Farmers Home Administration, successor to the Farm Security Administration, an agency set up within the Department of Agriculture. It attempts to help the economically poorer farmers in a variety of ways. When it discovers a farmer on a good acreage of land but without enough equipment or capital to make a go, it arranges for the refunding of his indebtedness and lends him sufficient money to equip his farm with such stock and machinery as will make it profitable. A part of this procedure is the working out of a careful plan for that specific farm with the supervisors of the FHA. The plan not only deals with acreages of commercial crops, numbers of livestock, and the like, but includes detailed steps for making the farm family more self-sufficient through gardening, canning, and preserving.

The FSA operated a tenant purchase plan whereby skilled farmers were helped to purchase an adequately stocked and equipped acreage on terms which provide for amortization over a forty-year period. This plan had special reference to the cotton croppers of the South and was an attempt to establish capable individuals on their own holdings. Without some such system of aid it is almost impossible for a cropper to secure land or to hold it.

The FSA experimented with various types of co-operative farms in an attempt to adapt large-scale farming methods and machine production to ownership and control by the working farmer. Some of these experiments are most suggestive as to next steps in keeping farmers independent on rich land in the plain states, where machine operation of large acreages is the economical course. Under plans for co-operative ownership farmers band together and buy a large acreage of land, together with such equipment in tractors, plows, disks, and so forth as can operate that acreage most efficiently. They also purchase and own jointly a herd of cows for their own use and raise and butcher their meat animals co-operatively. By buying together they keep from bidding the price of land up as they would if each purchased a small acreage separately and in competition with the others. By operating together they avoid the inefficiencies of small operations and small machinery. It is to be hoped that experiments in this type of ownership and operation outside government supervision will be tried in order that the independent validity of the system may be known.

A most important element in the program of the FSA was the building and operation of government camps for migrant workers wherever these workers are found in force. Unquestionably the FSA has done more than any other agency to bring cleanliness, health, decent accommodations, and wholesome community relationships to migrant agricultural workers. Under its leadership standards have been set up for the treatment of migrant workers, and many of the attacks made upon the FSA by big-business interests in agriculture have been due to the fact that these same interests have had to approximate FSA standards to secure migrant labor. Both the co-operative farms and the migrant camps were closed by order of Congress in 1946 when it established the Farmers Home Administration as successor to the Farm Security Administration.

Economic welfare: the nonfarmer

What of the nonfarmer in rural life? There is good evidence to indicate that in a major depression his plight is apt to be worse than that of the farmer. The village industrial worker is first to be laid off if times are bad and last to be rehired when production is resumed, because industrial concerns first close their outlying plants and continue operations as long as possible in central plants in or near large cities. The coal miner suffers with depressions because coal is so deeply enmeshed in the general economic life of our country. When industries close down, their requirements for coal drastically diminish, and there is widespread suffering throughout the coal camps.

The first court of appeal for rural people faced with hunger is the local relief office, which may be on a village, township, or county basis. Whatever the arrangement, the local supervisor of the poor will dole out an amount of money or credit sufficient to provide a meager sustenance for the family. Such minimum support comes from local or state funds, and the local authority is always on the lookout for ways and means of getting relief clients on the rolls of agencies with financial resources beyond the local area. Former agencies of the latter type were the various work-relief projects of the great depression, culminating in the Works Progress Administration. Able-bodied persons certified as in need were hired by this agency for public works at a wage set in the light of living costs in the particular locality. Thus while WPA common labor in southern Wisconsin received sixty dollars a month, northern Wisconsin workers received but forty. WPA laborers were also eligible for benefits from the Surplus Commodities Corporation; that is, the government bought up surplus fruits and vegetables to maintain the price for these farm products and distributed them free to relief clients and WPA workers as well as to certain of our non-relief low-income families.

The entire concept of work relief as giving a man socially necessary work to do when social factors take away his regular employment is one with which the enlightened Christian conscience must agree. Of the expression of this ideal in the WPA there must be criticism on at least two important grounds. The first is the inflexibility with which WPA rules were made and administered, particularly in the early days of the agency. Rules as to eligibility were so strict as to cause workers to refuse other temporary jobs because of the great difficulty in securing a WPA certification at the end of such temporary employment. Thus local employers had difficulty getting workers, while the WPA rolls were crowded. This is no reflection on the workers involved, for they had to think of the long-term security of their families. A three-weeks' harvest job would not see them through the winter, and they did not dare face the chance of a winter without WPA wages.

A second criticism of WPA grows out of this first. Because it did not reflect the thinking and attitude of local people, it made the physical extremity of the unemployed worker the occasion for his alienation from the community. When he refused regular, though temporary, employment to keep his WPA job, he affronted the standards of his own community. The funds and the work which were supposed to help him maintain his morale became the necessities which drove him into actions and attitudes separating him from his fellows. Thus WPA programs became in many communities a means of class division between those who maintained the old ways and attitudes and those who took WPA employment. More consideration of local communities and their attitudes in establishing requirements and administering the program would have helped to maintain community solidarity.

Categorical aids

But rural persons in economic distress because of natural cataclysm or general economic depression do not exhaust the category of persons to be helped by welfare programs. There remain those suffering from a variety of handicaps, assistance to whom is classified under the term "categorical aids." Categorical aids include all kinds of assistance granted to the aged, the blind, the deaf, the crippled, dependent children, widows, and veterans. Such aids are granted in a variety of ways: medical attention is always given; regular payments for current living expenses may be granted; special educational needs may be met; special equipment for overcoming a handicap may be supplied. These aids vary greatly from state to state, and the pastor should consult the county relief office or the state department of public welfare to see exactly what is offered in his particular state. He has a real function to perform here, inasmuch as many people working under handicaps do not know of the help available to them.

In addition to these categorical aids, administered largely in the homes of the handicapped persons, there are special ministries offered under state supervision to particular classes of sufferers. Here may be listed homes for feeble-minded children, mental hospitals, sanatoria for tubercular patients, cancer clinics, and institutions for the delinquent. The pastor owes it to his people to acquaint himself, by personal visitation, with such institutions as these to which his people are or may be referred. He ought to help his people rid themselves of the dread with which many of us unfortunately picture such institutions. When a child in a family shows signs of being feeble-minded, the pastor can explain to parents that they, in sending such a child to a special state-supported school for his care, are making available to him the advantages which he can best use. Similarly, we should work to overcome the feeling of shame so often connected with mental hospitals; a broken mind may be as little the patient's own fault as a broken leg, and it requires the same careful treatment. Such treatment is available for most of our people only at the state institution for the care of the insane.

The modern state under the domination of the concept of public welfare has given us aids, services, and institutions specially devised to meet every kind of distress and handicap. As yet many of our people are not prepared to take advantage of these resources; pride or shame, both equally false, prevent them from securing for their loved ones the very real help and permanent assistance to be had for the asking. The challenge to the pastor and to the church is so to interpret these services to our people by public statement, group discussion, and pastoral counsel that they will see in them, not a cause for shame, but an avenue toward health and usefulness.

It is now almost a generation since the original Social Security Act established the Old-Age and Survivors Insurance program. In it our federal government set itself to the task of anticipating the emergencies of old age and bereavement and of building an adequate reserve through payroll taxes for the meeting of them. The early Act did not affect rural people except as they were industrially employed, for farmers, farm laborers, and the self-employed were specifically excluded. But the years have seen a steady increase not only in Social Security benefits but in coverage as well. Farm laborers and even many migrants are now covered. Farmers, small-town businessmen, and even the preacher may now be covered under the special category of self-employed persons. It is certainly more in keeping with the dignity of free men to be given a means of providing against life's vicissitudes in common with one's fellow citizens than to run the risk of becoming dependent upon public support when emergencies arise. In the Old-Age and Survivors Insurance program, the government has developed a technique for making self-help effective in the impersonality of a mass society.

12

THE SOCIAL-CLASS SYSTEM

THUS FAR we have dealt with the spatial patterns in which rural persons are related to one another, the reactions and agencies that stem out of their common dependence upon natural resources, the organizations and institutions which arise in the meeting of the several needs that rural persons share. This complex of relationships is the rural community. But persons in community are related to one another in still another fashion. They take or are assigned positions of superiority and inferiority in community preference. It is extremely difficult for Americans and churchmen to understand and to accept this fact. As Americans we constantly remind ourselves that "all men are created equal." As churchmen we remember that "there is neither Jew nor Greek, there is neither slave nor free, there is neither male nor female; for you are all one in Christ Jesus" (Galatians 3:28, R.S.V.). Written deeply into our minds and consciences is the conviction that all men are equal in the sight of God and of the state. The inequality and consequent inequities of our modern rural society are ignored because we so deeply need to believe in equality.

Since 1937 a series of careful studies has demonstrated the fact that a social-class system does exist in ordinary rural communities. If you ask a number of citizens in almost any rural community whether there exists a class system where they live, you can depend upon a solidly negative answer. "Here we are all alike," "We're just one big, happy family," and "We don't have any aristocrats here," are some of the responses you will get. But if you have provided yourself with a sample list of citizens of the community, with each name typed on a separate card, and if you then ask these same informants to take the fifty or sixty cards and put people who are alike together, you will get an astonishing reversal of the negative. After a few preliminary shuffles through the cards, they will begin to lay them out in three piles. One small pile will be designated as high-class or quality people; a second and the largest pile will be made up of good, steady, hard-working people; a third pile, somewhat larger than the first, will contain the shiftless and no-good crowd. There may be some variation around this basic threefold classification with divisions made within the second and third piles. What is significant, however, is that whether the particular person making the classifications is himself placed high or low, he will tend to agree with other informants both as to where the general run of people are placed and as to where he himself belongs.

Measuring social status

To discover the class system of a particular community by this method is to use the plan of "rating by matched agreements" described by Warner, Meeker, and Eells in *Social Class in America*. These authors have perfected an "index of status characteristics" which a student can apply to the citizens of a community without depending upon the subjective appraisal of others. Ratings are given to an individual on his occupation, source of income, house type, and dwelling area. Then these ratings, properly weighted, are added to provide an over-all index of status. The index has a potential range of 12 to 84. The lower the index, the higher the status of the person involved. The student who wishes to use this method of analysis should make a careful study of *Social Class in America* and the monographic studies of American communities on which it is based.

Wherever careful community studies have been made, a social-class system has been found to exist; that is, the people of the community are consistently regarded by their fellows as occupying positions of relatively greater or less prestige, authority, and power. It is not this fact by itself that gives us concern but the conditions that flow from it and the way in which it affects the church. It is clearly demonstrated by many studies that the commonly created goods of our social order are not equally distributed. The higher the class position of an individual, the more he gets; the lower the class position, the less he gets.

A. B. Hollingshead, in *Elmtown's Youth,* has given us a study of an American county-seat high school in action. His study shows that upper-class and upper-middle-class boys and girls received over twice the proportion of grades 85 and above which they should have had by chance alone; whereas the lower-lower-class students received only a third of the high grades they might have expected. Clearly some bias is at work here. It might be argued that higher intelligence goes with higher status and accounts for the difference. It is true that the higher-class youth showed higher intelligence, but not to the extent that would explain the difference in grades. Apparently the lower down in the social-class system a boy or girl is, the less is expected of him by his teachers. His inability to do good work is taken for granted, and he is permitted to flunk courses without remonstrance. But an upper-class student, if his work begins to deteriorate, is reminded by his teachers that he is a good student, that he is expected to pass his courses as a preliminary to going on to college. Special help is extended to him in after-school tutoring sessions and special opportunities given him to make up exams which he has failed. At the end of the term he gets a "B" whether on merit or not. His lower-class brother gets an "F."

The same situation exists in terms of law enforcement. Juveniles who run athwart the law, if they come from the families of the elite, are given a polite reprimand and taken home to their parents. But the boy from the wrong side of the tracks spends his night in jail. Equality before the law is a basic principle of our American life, but such equality is not equality before the law enforcers. Men assigned the task of maintaining order do not note the crime first; they note the criminal. And if the malefactor comes from a reputable enough family, they condone his actions and mitigate any penalty insofar as they can.

We churchmen dare not sanctimoniously condemn these other public servants. To begin with, they are not acting purposely in this fashion; they are simply giving practical expression to community attitudes which lie largely hidden and consciously unexpressed in our minds. Certain families seem to us so superior as to be incapable of failure or wrongdoing. Indeed, they so symbolize our community values that to admit their failure or transgression would be to question the whole ordered fabric of our common life. Other families are equally associated with lack of ambition, inferiority, failure, and the transgression of community standards. We expect nothing much from them—indeed, are surprised when they meet even minimum standards of conduct. If we commonly share such attitudes, should we wonder that such official representatives of the community as the teacher and the policeman should act upon them?

The church and social class

Furthermore, in the churches the class system comes to one of its most definite expressions. The various studies of social class indicate that the churches tend to become identified with the several classes. Denominations vary in their class position from region to region. In one rural community in central Indiana farm owners go to the Methodist church, farm renters to the Presbyterian church, and farm laborers to the Assembly of God. In a New England hill town the elite attend the Congregational church, the middle class are Methodist, the lower-middle and lower class Roman Catholic. Other situations would produce other relative ratings. The important consideration is that churches do not serve the various strata of the population equally but tend to serve one or another class.

This fact is sometimes used as an excuse for not attempting to secure the membership and participation of lower-class persons in middle-class churches. The argument runs: "Don't worry about them, the Holy Rollers will take care of the poor. They wouldn't be happy in our formal church services. They want action, noise, and emotion. Let the revivalistic sects take care of them." Now it is true that the revivalistic sects draw their memberships largely from the lower classes; but the inference cannot be made that the lower classes are comprehensively or effectively served by these fellowships. All the data we can amass indicates that the lower down in the social scale a person or family is, the less the chance that they will belong to or participate in any church at all. Sewell's data on eight hundred Oklahoma farm families given in Table III of Chapter 3 indicates that the poorer the family, the less likely the husband or wife to participate in any church. Hollingshead deals with this situation in discussing Class V (the lower-lower class) characteristics in *Elmtown's Youth*. He shows that only 71 per cent of the families in this class indicate any sort of ecclesiastical connection, that 98 per cent of the fathers and 90 per cent of the mothers are either not known by any local minister or known not to attend church. Harold F. Kaufman in a study of *Prestige Classes in a New York Rural Community* discovered that 78 per cent of the persons in his prestige classes 1-2 were active church members, but that only 1 per cent of the persons in his classes 4.5-6 were active church members. Whether it be in a village in rural New York State, in a county-seat town in northern Illinois, or among farm families in widely scattered sections of Oklahoma, the lower in the social scale a person is, the less the chance that he will belong to or participate in *any* church.

In the face of such facts, we should give up the excuse that we need not be concerned with lower-class people because the emotionalistic sects will care for them. Such sects just are not caring for them. An approach that enlists less than ten per cent participation on the part of a whole category of persons deserves no serious consideration. What we must do is to recover a sense of the value of persons in themselves, of man's basic dignity everywhere and in all conditions as a child of God and our brother. Such an attitude would make impossible the condescension implied above.

Christians will generally admit that the differential presentation of the gospel is a bad thing which we must pray and work to overcome. But this is not the only serious personal cost we pay for the social-class system. If lower-class youth get a poorer education because of their inferior status, then society is the loser, because these young people are not being educated up to the excellent abilities which many of them have. No society has too much of intelligence and leadership, and any social process or condition which prevents the development of such intelligence and leadership is bad. What we sometimes observe is that such an arrangement is "bad luck" for the young man or woman so treated; what we must quickly see is that it is "bad luck" for all of us. We need to develop all the latent talent we can wherever we find it.

Again, many of us are upwardly mobile persons in the class structure. We began in a relatively humble position; and by education, hard work, ambition, and "the breaks" we have moved to a superior status. Perhaps our parents were farm renters, but we had a taste for knowledge and their loyal support. We made our way through high school, college, and university; and now we are serving in some professional capacity in the rural community. We may be superintendent of schools, farm adviser, soil-conservation district technician, pastor of the county-seat church. In these positions we are manifestly higher in the social scale than we began. Such upward movement means that we and our families move socially in circles where standards of manners are different from those we learned as children. We attempt to conform to those standards, to show that we are old hands at it, always haunted with an inner fear that we will do the wrong thing, make some blunder that will alienate from us the fine new friends. In our work we are constantly reminded of the pressure of young men and women coming up behind us. Will we maintain our newly established position of prestige and even advance a bit, or will we slip back into the humble status from which we came? Much of the anxiety we note in our lives from day to day results from the functioning of the social-class system.

That there are differences of capacity and temperament among persons, we would all agree. Such differences, we should expect, would result in positions of varying authority and responsibility in any complex social order. Any society needs leaders and followers; it needs specialists to whom it gives honor and recognition because of the importance of the contributions they make to the general welfare. But what is required is that persons of equal ability should have an equal opportunity to train and equip themselves for service to the commonweal. If we as Americans take the Declaration of Independence seriously or as Christians take our common sonship to a single Father in heaven to heart, we shall become increasingly restless under our current practice and more and more determined to reform it.

Class and caste

You may have read the foregoing with a question as to why no mention has been made of the caste system of race and color that affects rural Americans in so many ways. Negroes, Mexicans, Spanish Americans, Indians, Chinese, Japanese, all live as something less than full citizens in certain sections of our country. Differences of skin color often keep our fellow Americans from enjoying full educational opportunity, decent protection by the police, the use of such public facilities as parks, beaches, playgrounds, and theaters. This denial of equal participation to Americans on any physical grounds is a shameful thing not only because it thwarts the individual but also because it denies the nation the best use of the abilities he possesses. The same personal results that we have ascribed to the social-class system are produced by racial discrimination as well.

I have given first consideration and emphasis here to class discrimination because it is a much more pervasive and subtle reality. Americans are aware of the facts of racial discrimination and are making advances in eliminating it. But most of us are not aware of class discrimination, and we need to be alerted to this serious internal threat to our common peace and happiness, this subversion of basic Christian and American attitudes. Christians should certainly not give any less attention or effort to overcoming race prejudice; but they must become aware of the similar injustices which flow from our class system. The way to complete justice and equality is a hard, perhaps an impossible, one, but we cannot take our first halting steps along it until we come under conviction of sin where class bias is concerned. God made us to be free and equal, and the social inequities we have described are at once an affront to his purpose and a denial of our own basic nature as his children.

13

THE COMMUNITY—AN OPPORTUNITY FOR THE CHURCH

THROUGHOUT OUR discussion we have been concerned with an understanding of the community and its agencies in order that the church might serve them more effectively. Surely there is no debate as to the responsibility the church bears to serve the community from which it draws its life. What we as pastors are apt to forget all too often, however, is that the service relation between church and community is not one-sided. The church should and must serve its community, but the community just as really does serve the church. To forget this is to be guilty of lack of appreciation of the gifts the rural community offers us.

The community as source of our human material

First of all, as I have pointed out again and again, the community supplies the human material with which the church must work. To the degree in which the homes and the schools of the community are excellent they provide the church a fitting foundation on which to build the mature structure of personality. The religious life customarily uses a series of family metaphors: God is our *Father,* so what we have come to know about fatherhood in our own family conditions our possible relationship to God; men are our *brothers* and our *neighbors,* so that what brotherhood and neighborliness mean in our community becomes background for our understanding of the Christian good news. A community in which all agencies work to strengthen family and school has rendered a priceless service to the Christian church.

The community defining our responsibility

The community also serves the church in setting a framework within which the effectiveness of church work may be judged. The community has definite limits, a definite population, definite classes of persons. These measurable items of community life, as we have seen in Chapter 3, become standards to which the church must bring its achievement for judgment. A church which meets its budget, has a respectable membership, and pays a decent salary is likely to become self-satisfied and think that it is a successful church. What we need is a standard for measurement outside ourselves whereby we can determine our success or failure, and we find this standard in the community. No church is a successful church in a Christian sense if there are areas in its community where people are unserved by a Christian congregation or if there are classes to whom the gospel is not preached. The community faces us with the area and the persons for whom we are responsible as ministers of God.

Are there too many churches in our town, or are we underchurched? This question cannot be answered in terms of a village or a township alone. Only in terms of the developing town-country community can we explore the relationship of church organizations to need and detect the presence of too many churches in our midst or the need for more. Often what we have considered as overchurching has been rather a focusing of too much attention on the people in the village center. What many churches need to do is to go out into the countryside where the fields are white unto the harvest and the laborers few. Community-mindedness emancipates us from slavery to the village center.

The community as administrative unit

Concerned denominational officials will find in the community a rational basis for circuit organization. Again and again we hear the complaint with regard to churches yoked in circuits: "We can put them together, but we cannot make them work together." Of course that is what we ought logically to expect if we join churches for pastoral service without any regard to their community relationships. If people from Jones Creek and Spike Hill neighborhoods do not trade and learn and play together, it is scarcely to be expected that they will pray together with any particular enthusiasm or reality. To be effective in anything more than a formal sense, circuits must be arranged within the limits of a single community area.

The community as arena for Christian action

The chief contribution that the rural community has to make to the church, however, is in the opportunity it offers to the church to be fully Christian. Within the rural community man faces a society which has not yet grown too large or too complex to be manageable. To say this is not to argue that rural communities can be or should strive to be entirely self-sufficient or to deny the participation of rural society as a whole in the network of interrelationships which make up modern civilization. What is insisted upon here is the fact, often lost sight of, that in the rural community it is still possible for one to know all the community members personally and to base every relationship within the community on personal consideration and a sense of personal responsibility. Not that this is done very often, but it can be done.

And unless it is done, not once or in an isolated situation, but again and again, the chance that our world situation will grow toward peace and personal security is hopelessly remote. In the rural community we have a microcosm reflecting all the strains and frictions we sense in the macrocosm which is our world, but in the rural community we meet these strains and frictions on a personal and face-to-face basis. If the Christian will cannot bring order and satisfaction out of social strife among rural citizens of the community in our day, if the local pastor cannot lead his people in their town in the way of peace, then all our talk about the church's leading our world into a just and durable peace is talk and nothing more. "He that loveth not his brother whom he hath seen, how can he love his brother whom he hath not seen?" we might urge in adapting and re-applying John's noble argument.

And this is seen to be all the more true when we remember that the rural community is educating the citizens of the cities of tomorrow. Unless the spirit of Christian forbearance, toler-ance, and sacrifice dominates not simply their thinking but their successful experience in solving social problems at home, dare we believe that they will develop these needed qualities in the rush and tension of city life? If greed succeeds in the rural community, then it will be tried more and more in the city; if intolerance is effective in promoting selfish enjoyment in rural community life, then we can expect bigger and better pogroms in the cities of the future. The rural pastor from day to day is cultivating those attitudes and experiences which are fraught with fateful import for all civilization tomorrow. Today in race riots in Detroit or Chicago we see the failure of the rural church in Georgia or North Carolina or Illinois to measure up to its community opportunity yesterday.

In the arena of its community the church faces conflict. Community conflict is involved when an issue arises on which the greater part of the community takes sides so that the minds of the people are engaged in devising programs to defeat one another rather than in promoting the welfare of all. It is ob-vious that this sort of conflict threatens the stability of common living itself. Not only are people made unhappy when they are thus arrayed against one another, but valuable mental and physical resources which might be used to meet real problems are dissipated in bickering and contravention.

Conflict is not to be regarded as totally bad, however, for

it calls our attention to neglected interests of the people of a community. Most such conflicts arise because the fundamental needs of a group of persons are not being met. Conflict may begin between occupational categories: the farmer may suspect the villager, the villager look down upon the farmer. It may arise between structural levels within the community: the neighborhood may feel its identity threatened by the larger community, as in the whole matter of school consolidation, for example. Age groups may be involved: youth against maturity is one case, often in conflict over the recreation question. Community agencies and institutions may fight one another, as the church, the school, or the Grange against the Community Club. And agencies of the same kind may fight one another. Perhaps this is the most bitter type of community conflict— denomination fighting with denomination, club with club. Such conflicts arise in all communities, but there are special conflict situations which demand our attention: conflict between Negro and white, conflict between migrant and settled farmer, conflict between organized or organizing labor and management. These last special cases ought to be in the forefront of our attention as we discuss community conflict, for they represent new types of social alignment which may characterize rural life more and more.

What shall the church do in conflict situations? The temptation is to take Pilate's course and wash our hands of the whole business. We are men of peace and should not be expected to become embroiled in such bitterness. One pastor boasted that while there had been an open conflict in his town for five years, he had succeeded in keeping it out of the church. Of course he was deluding himself. He had not kept it out of the church, for it was a reality day and night in the lives of his church members. He had prevented it from coming to open expression in a church meeting. But what price had he paid for such exemption from the strife engulfing the whole community? He had made religion irrelevant to daily life, so that men and women could rise and work and live in that community with hearts full of hatred yet never feel the judgment of a loving God upon what they were doing.

Most of us feel that this is too heavy a price to pay. We are convinced that the church ought to have a message for the conflict, yet we are faced with the difficulty of finding a satisfactory technique for registering a Christian protest and effecting a Christian reconciliation. We want to do something, but without a plan we let the conflict go on so that our neglect becomes in the end as disastrous as our brother's calculated neutrality. Here is our great opportunity; here is a chance to build for peace and world community at the grass roots. It is safe to say that, unless we can develop a spirit of peace and a machinery for the amicable settlement of differences in our home towns, we can scarcely hope to build a world system of peace in our day.

The church facing conflict

First of all, then, let the church bring the conflict out into the open. Not that the pastor should do this obviously or brusquely, save in the most extreme situations, but he should follow up allusions to the conflict as they come out in church-school board, in prayer meeting, in official board, and indicate that the conflict is a proper subject for Christian discussion. In all such discussions of the conflict, the pastor should attempt to view the situation impartially and to get his people so to do. This should be true even—perhaps we should say particularly—when the church itself is a party to the conflict. What case has the other side? Are we doing its point of view justice as we talk about the matter? Are we fighting it, or the construct of our own imagination?

When the conflict has been brought out into the open, then let the church seek to distinguish between the real and subsidiary issues. Once a conflict has arisen, it is always clouded by personal grudges or ancient animosities. These the church must clear away so that the real and significant difference becomes evident. Sometimes this is sufficient to dismiss the whole

165

matter as a live issue, for the conflict has been raised over dead issues because of personal rivalries. When people find this out, they automatically stop fighting, no matter how bellicose their leaders may continue to be. But whether this happens or not, when the main issue is isolated and clearly stated, the community is at last on the road to a vital solution.

A third step is to explore the possibility of substituting common interests for like interests. We may be said to have like interests when two persons or groups are seeking to secure something of which there is a limited amount, not enough to go around. When school and church become program centered in their outlook upon youth, then they may be said to have like interests. Their interest is in the specific programs they are promoting for the youth of the community. In most rural communities the limited number of young people to be served means that two vigorous and mutually exclusive programs must be competitive for the time and energy of the few youth available. But suppose we move from a concern for our particular program to a broader and more fundamental concern for the real welfare of young people. Then both school and church have a common interest. Then they cease to be competitors and become what ideally they must always be, the closest of allies. Our concern in every case of conflict within the community should be to comprehend the issue in such terms as will substitute a common interest for like interests.

When we have developed a common interest between the conflicting parties, there is a further step we must take if the breach really is to be healed: we must engage both parties in a specific common enterprise. Only when people are actually working together for a concrete end will the experience of conflict be completely and successfully overridden. This concrete common task should be a practical expression of their common interest. For instance, if school and church leaders are brought to see that their common interest is the welfare of youth, they may be challenged to clear together a convenient field and supply it with playground equipment. In such a program, we

may further note, it would be better to supply homemade playground equipment than to spend energy in earning money for
the purchase of such material. The best sort of cement for community solidarity is the experience of church and school leaders
in working side by side.

It would be hopelessly optimistic to suppose, however, that
all community conflict can be resolved in this fashion. As long
as there are injustices in our economic and social life, as long
as large numbers of our fellows are faced with unmet needs,
just so long community conflicts must continue to develop in
the interest of justice and human welfare. Such conflicts based
upon real differences must be solved if community life is to
continue to be possible.

First of all, we have to insist that repression presents no
solution to the conflict. The history of Negro-white relationships and of labor organization in the United States proves that
repressive measures lead only to retaliatory violence on the part
of the minority group against which they are directed. The immediate battle may be overwhelmingly won by the dominant
power, but the war is only embittered and prolonged by repressive tactics. The manager of a small New England factory
fired the man who he knew was attempting to organize his fellow
workers into a union. Inasmuch as this man was known by his
fellows to be one of the best workers, it was abundantly clear
to them that his discharge was due to his organizing activities,
though their employer claimed otherwise. They came to regard
this discharge as a direct challenge to them, so that they took
up with a personal interest the organizing campaign which their
unfortunate fellow workman had begun. Furthermore, either
purposely or because their minds were taken up with this disturbing affair, their production began to fall off and the quality
of their work to deteriorate. The manager met this production
slump, not with understanding, but with threats and then with
further firings. Under such procedure the men grew more sul-
len, more resentful, more suspicious, willingly believing all the
charges made against the manager, although many of these were

untrue. Within two years' time the factory was forced to suspend operations, the manager lost his job, and all the men were out of work. The original repressive attitude and acts of the manager eventually made impossible the co-operative enterprise in which he and his workmen were engaged.

Paternalism is an equally ineffective answer. The come-tell-me-about-it-and-I'll-fix-it-up-for-you approach is one which, in the long run, disgusts mature men and women. People living in company villages under such a tutelage are never grateful for the real benefits they receive, since they always suspect the company of some ulterior motive in supplying such comforts. The managership of the company, on the other hand, is always bitter at the lack of gratitude on the part of the workers for what the company does for them. Advantages thus supplied are quickly neglected by these for whom they are planned, since they are the result of neither the planning nor the work of the recipients. Any real physical or economic good achieved by paternalistic domination is more than overbalanced by the fact that such good is not the free choice and achievement of persons involved. The unhappy fate of the American Indian under the guardianship of the federal government should be an object lesson in the inadequacy of paternalism to produce free and integrated personalities and a self-sustaining community life.

The church as channel of communication

The first step in a vital approach toward the solution of community conflict of a fundamental sort lies in keeping open channels of communication between potentially conflicting groups. Differences between groups are never dangerous so long as there exists a common agency through which the parties to the difference may communicate. It is when the parties have no longer any way of speaking to one another that violence is apt to break out. Both parties say: "There is nothing left to do but fight." Situations of racial tension furnish one example of conflict in which the church ought to strive to keep open an avenue of communication. In this light we may see the action of a Virginia ministerial association in establishing itself on an inter-racial basis as essentially wise and Christian. There now exists in that county one agency in which white and black can meet to communicate to one another their needs and points of view.

The church itself should be always such an agency of inter-communication. In it people of every race, occupation, and class should find a sympathetic home. Evidence introduced in Chapters 3 and 12 indicating that the church does not attract people of the poorer economic levels as much as it does those of the richer is disturbing not only to those who love the church but to all who seek for social understanding and peace. The church ideally speaks to and for people of every condition; any policy or program which makes it the instrument of a particular class or point of view is not only unfortunate for the church but unfortunate for the social fabric as a whole. Each pastor should have as a conscious aim of his whole ministry the reaching of every sort of person with the fellowship of the church.

Since different churches appeal in varying degree to people of diverse economic levels in the population, it is essential that churchmen recognize this fact and seek through their ministerial associations to build a group representing all types of people. An informal pastors' association is always possible, and in this the Roman Catholic and the Synodical Conference Lutheran can co-operate without disobeying any of the regulations of their respective churches. It is important for pastors of the freer churches to understand that worship with other Christians is specifically forbidden to pastors in some denominations. Common prayer ought not to be the first approach to co-operation among church groups. Most of us sin by attempting to go too far and too fast in these matters; a good first step is simply to achieve a consultative meeting of pastors once a month.

Particular care must be taken to get representation on ministerial associations from the churches which work especially with the poorer classes. We need not fear that opening our organization membership to the "holiness" preachers will dignify their theology or practice in the eyes of the populace or bring them a larger following. As a matter of fact, opposition to them is always interpreted by the man in the street as an expression of the jealousy of the professional toward the layman's effectiveness. Studies indicate again and again that through these leaders the unevangelized multitude speaks, and it is important that all of us should know what that multitude is saying.

The fact that we are pastors of "respectable" churches and congregations is apt to lead us to a one-sidedness in assessing the right and wrong of any controversy between social groups. The leaders of the underprivileged may not please us, and we will be tempted to reject their pleas for justice because we do not like their manners. We must learn to hear a man on the specific point at issue. It is easy to disregard the justice of a labor leader's arguments if we know that he drinks a glass of whisky now and then. We must learn that a man may be wrong on whisky but right on hours and pay in a textile plant. Hitler and Mussolini were both total abstainers, but this fact does not lead us to accept their judgment on social matters. Neither should another man's indulgence lead us to turn a deaf ear to his arguments.

How do we serve as an agency of intercommunication? Suppose farmers in our area begin to experiment with the raising of sugar beets and, as a result of this new agricultural enterprise, Mexican families begin to come to our village to tend the beets. The Mexicans are readily identifiable on our streets; their dark complexions, their strange attire, their volubility in a strange language, all mark them off as outsiders. Their different work habits, developed in a semitropical climate, which require that they take an occasional holiday, whatever may be the convenience or inconvenience of such a work stoppage to their employer, will cause us to regard them as lazy or unambitious. It will be easy for us to shrug off any religious responsibility for them by insisting that they are Roman Catholics and not interested in anything we have to offer. Thus the stage is all set for the relegation of the Mexicans to a definitely low-caste position in our community as something less than full human beings. Of course, economic interest will then make it easy to argue that such creatures do not deserve the pay or the accommodations of full human beings. When we have housed them in dirty shacks, provided them with no sanitary conveniences or opportunities for bathing, and paid them peon wages, we can point to their slovenly living conditions as proof positive that our early hunch as to their subhuman character was right.

All this is possible to people who at the same time prate about the importance of the Good Neighbor policy in Mexico. But that the Good Neighbor policy will ever result in anything more than polite and pious conversation is quite unlikely so long as neighborliness to Mexicans at home is carried on as we have described it. A serious responsibility devolves upon us as churchmen here, a responsibility at once requiring tact and boldness. People must be made to see for themselves that Mexicans are people. They must experience individual Mexicans as friends, persons for whom they hold respect and affection. Then any discussion of the Good Neighbor policy will be realistic and promising.

A pastor in a central Michigan community was faced with this particular problem. He himself had offered his personal friendship to the Mexicans, had become their sponsor and spokesman on more than one occasion, knew them and their problems well. His church members, however, were not so well acquainted with Mexicans and hence much readier with criticism. One man insisted that the Mexicans were loading the relief-agency rolls and becoming an increasing burden to the county. Knowing that Mexican family life is based on a pattern of responsibility for all members, collateral as well as blood, the pastor challenged this uninformed critic to check the relief rolls with him. Together at the welfare office they went through the lists; over halfway they went without discovering a single Mexican name; then they came to the Manuelo family. After it there were no others—one Mexican family receiving public assistance in the whole county. Interested in understanding this particular case, the pastor and his friend went to the leader among the Mexicans, with whom he had most friendly relationships. "How does it happen that the Manuelo family is getting relief?" he asked. "Oh, those Manuelos," sighed the Mexican friend, "I guess they are getting too Americanized."

Such words, more than any argument, brought home to the critical church member the unrealistic analysis that Mexicans might make of Americans with as much fairness as he had applied in forming his opinion of Mexicans. Failure to understand breeds failure to understand. Only personal acquaintance, first-hand knowledge, can help us to form adequate opinions of one another. When Mexicans enter the community, then, the pastor should make their acquaintance, but he should never leave it at that. He should see to it that lay men and women make their acquaintance as well. He should be on the lookout for someone with a knowledge of Spanish, in order that he may communicate with them in their own language. Going to a man on his own terms is one of the best ways of really understanding him. Summer vacation child-care centers, provision of adequate public toilet and bathing facilities where Mexican families are camping out, social evenings together with entertainment provided by Mexican singers themselves—all these and other services that the imaginative Christian can devise will implement the Good Neighbor policy at the place where it affects the taproots of American public attitude.

The church as champion of objectivity

According to our Master, it is only as we know the truth that we become free. Therefore as pastors we must stand always on the side of truth. Our business is to seek and to disclose the facts behind any community controversy, to let the light of truth point the road to freedom. And this involves two tasks: one a continual study of our community, that we may sense the trends that affect its life and observe new facts as they develop, the other a special study of the issues in specific disputes within the community in order that we may have a factual basis for declaring what is fair and just.

An objective concern for truth is particularly important when the church itself is party to a conflict. Recently a church in a northern Illinois village found itself embroiled with the neighbor adjoining the parsonage property over the location of the parsonage garage. According to the neighbor's calculations, the garage was two feet over on his property, and he demanded that the church take action in clearing his land of the building. The structure was such that there could be no question of moving it entire to another location; any moving of the garage involved its total dismemberment and reconstruction.

Within the church and community there was a strong sentiment in favor of fighting the case legally and securing the rights of the church on the basis of customary use if no other. The pastor, however, rightly sensed that any such standing upon abstract right would be fatal to the ministry of the church. With a specially appointed committee he studied the village plan and had a new survey made which demonstrated that the neighbor's statement of his case was accurate and the church actually in the wrong. The committee then recommended to the official board that the church remove the offending garage, not because the neighbor made such a demand, but because it was the right and fair thing to do. The official board voted to take this action, and the men of the church began the process.

When the community as a whole saw what the church was planning to do, the reaction was immediate and powerful. Men who had previously been indifferent to the claims of religion understood that here was a church in which religion dominated the action of the people. They volunteered in numbers to assist in rebuilding the garage. The suggestion was made that, since this reconstruction was to take place, the proper time was at hand for a complete replanning of the church and parsonage lots in terms of beauty and utility. The new plan caught the imagination of the people, and they offered money, time, and material for carrying it out. In the end the church and parsonage property became the outstanding group of buildings in the village. And many of those who had formerly been indifferent became concerned members of the Christian fellowship, because they had seen a demonstration of Christian loyalty to truth in the life of the church fellowship itself. A pastor and people loyal to truth turned a costly and seemingly unnecessary property adjustment into a demonstration of Christian consideration and helpfulness.

There is a fashion today, among Christians as well as in the world, to describe community life as a struggle for power and to express skepticism about the effectiveness of reason and good will in perfecting our social relationships. That irrational and unconscious motivations have their way in all of us is clear. But this recognition should not discourage us in our attempt to bring all motivation to the bar of reason nor permit us to relax into a subhuman truce with bigotry and selfishness. The Christian doctrine of the Holy Spirit suggests that the Spirit of God works with our spirits—there is something in us that the goodness and love of God can and does reach. If the divine Spirit is to move as a saving power among the "powers" of community life, it will move through the intelligence and good will of men like ourselves. We should never identify the perfection of God's Spirit with our plans for community betterment or allow pride in particular achievements to destroy our humility; but neither should we entertain a stultifying doubt as to his power to use us in the redemption of the common life. What our age needs is more and better sense applied to our immediate problems on the one hand, and on the other, a deeper faith in God and in our power to do what he commands.

14

COMMUNITY ORGANIZATION

OUR DISCUSSION thus far brings to sharp focus two seemingly contradictory facts: the rural community is served by so many organizations and agencies that duplication of effort is almost inevitable; at the same time there are interests and needs of large categories of persons within the community which are not being met and which, because unmet, are a seedbed for community dissension and conflict. To use a concrete illustration, here is a village of five hundred persons with five weak and struggling churches competing against one another. Because of such duplication of efforts they require an unusually high per-capita support from those who participate in their services, while, at the same time and for the same reason, they cannot enlist participation by many in the community who are sympathetic to a thoughtful and morally alive religion. In this same village youth is finding its recreational life in a commercial resort operated in connection with a tavern. Too much of the energy and resources of the community are being invested in a church life which in many ways denies the cause of true religion, while resources are not available for the adequate service of youth.

To remedy such a situation—that is, to prevent competition and duplication of services within the community while meeting real needs—is the purpose of community organization. Such organization works on the premise that the community is, in many important ways, a unit. It takes the community rather than the agency or individual point of view. It interprets the school, the church, the club, not in terms of separate and un-related programs, each existing in its own right, but rather as activities whose meaning is found in a common life. When a young pastor used in his publicity the phrase "the church as a community activity in Elwood," he was taking the viewpoint of community organization. The agencies of the community are essential to and support one another. In competition or open conflict all lose, no matter which one wins the temporary victory.

But how are we to work together? Good will alone is not enough at this point. Often we have had only the best intentions toward one another and a firm resolve to work together. Pastor and high-school coach feel at one in their common service to youth. Then the recreational program at the high school, warming up through the winter basketball season, begins to pre-empt more and more nights during the week. The climax comes when a special game is announced for the very night when the youth fellowship at the church has planned its midwinter banquet. With speaker engaged, arrangements perfected with the women of the church for serving supper, invitations out to surrounding youth groups, we can scarcely alter our plans. Yet half the boys on the team are members of our youth group and eager to be both places at once. And the coach, enmeshed in the mid-season enthusiasm and passions of basketball, is not inclined to be reasonable. The game goes through and so does the banquet. The boys on the team, nervous at best at this special test, are made more jittery by the feeling that they are failing their friends in the youth fellowship. They play poor basketball and lose the game. As for the banquet, it lacks that spark of zest which comes when the crowd is all together doing one thing enthusiastically, the stunts lack their usual punch, singing drags, and the speaker is faced with an apathetic audience. Even when we blame the coach for the failure of our plans, we cannot but sympathize with him as he blames us for the loss of a crucial game. Certainly afterward pastor and coach do not love and respect each other to a marked degree. The good will with which they began the year is decidely tarnished, and each one says under his breath, "After all, how can you work with a guy like that?"

A lost game, a spoiled banquet, misunderstanding and dislike between two influential community leaders—all this is bad. But it all seems much worse days later when we learn that on the night in question the village constable caught three of the junior-high-school boys pillaging the candy supplies in a soft-drink stand at the edge of town. While leaders are competing for the time and energy of a few young people, others are getting into serious trouble for want of an adult leader to be concerned about them. Is not this the situation we find ourselves facing again and again: school, church, and other community agencies competing among themselves and failing to meet real human needs within their community because, in spite of good intentions, they have no tried plan for working together at community tasks?

The community calendar

There are ways in which agencies within the community can reduce and eliminate duplication of effort and conflict of dates at the same time that they meet total needs more completely. The simplest of these is the community calendar. Basically this involves the use of a calendar or datebook in which the regular meeting dates and the special-event dates of all agencies and organizations within the community are recorded. Once a year, preferably in the late summer, a committee, perhaps composed of high-school and grade-school principals and the ministers, asks each organization to furnish it with a list of dates it wishes to reserve during the fall, winter, and spring months. These dates are then recorded on the calendar, any potential conflicts ironed out, and the calendar deposited in some public place where it is readily available to all. If plans for a specific activity are canceled, the listing is removed from the calendar. If new activities are developed, they are listed on the calendar upon open dates. All agencies agree not to schedule major activities on nights already pre-empted for other purposes. This does not mean, of course, that committee meetings of different organizations cannot be scheduled for the same night when there is no overlapping of membership. It does mean that no organization will put on a program for which it expects community support on a night already taken for some kindred activity.

Such a calendar may be handled quite informally. In Belchertown, Massachusetts, Editor Lewis Blackmer of the Belchertown *Sentinel* keeps such a record of plans and programs in his office. Month by month he lists coming events in a special column in the weekly *Sentinel*. At the beginning of the autumn season organizations submit their plans to him, and he enters the dates in question on his calendar. During the year a committee planning some special event always calls Mr. Blackmer to see if the date is clear before finally setting the time. If he reports some activity on the suggested date, the committee at once sets to work to find another appropriate one. There is an unwritten rule—indeed, it is a matter of good taste—that one organization will not trespass on the time of another.

In other communities the datebook is kept by the secretary of the superintendent of schools, and in his office. Occasionally the calendar is left at the post office in the care of the postmaster. The custodianship of the calendar is a minor affair, so long as it is in a place readily available to all and where there is someone generally present to take care of the necessary adjustments. Such a calendar once accepted by the community at large is almost completely self-enforcing. Should an organization break over the line and stage a community-wide event on the date reserved for another organization, the community as a whole is likely to indicate its disapproval by failure to patronize the competing event. Two or three rebuffs of this kind are enough to bring the most recalcitrant group into line.

The obvious advantages of such a plan in preventing duplication of effort, conflict over dates, and competition for support need not be argued. What is not so obvious is that such a calendar, by bringing together the total program of agencies within the community, enables us to see the blind spots in community life. A quick scanning of what is offered by all organizations within the community will disclose neglect of teen-age recreational needs or failure to provide interesting programs for young adults. Here is a summary audit of community effort and service which enables interested organizations so to reorient their programs as to meet the needs of neglected groups.

The community council

A more formal and comprehensive technique for community organization is offered in the community-council plan. A community council is a group constituted of representatives of all agencies in the community, which meets regularly to clear dates, to discuss needs and problems within the community, to develop plans for meeting such needs, and to assign responsibility for the carrying out of such plans to the member agencies. Such a council is ordinarily established by calling a meeting of representatives of all organizations under the guidance of an interested committee. At such a meeting the purpose of a community council is discussed, its method of acting is made clear, a simple constitution is suggested for reference back to the organizations represented, and a date is set for a confirming meeting of representatives when they have had time to get authority from their several groups. The constitution should provide a statement of purpose, rules for representation, time and place of meetings, order of business, officers, and plans of adoption.

Most councils provide for two representatives from each community group. Some meet once a month, while others find once a quarter adequate. All set a community calendar and revise it as is necessary from time to time. All begin by having several committees which survey the community as to health, recreation, care of children, and so on, to determine how adequately human needs are being met and what needs to be done to bring the community to a decent standard. Once the facts are known with regard to specific need or service, it becomes the duty of one of the standing committees to keep the information disclosed by the original study up to date and to suggest further actions which ought to be taken in the community.

How does such a council work? Let us take an example. At one of its regular meetings the Gompers Ferry Community Council is considering the report of its committee on recreation. The committee lists and describes the various recreational programs available in the community and then asks for correction or supplementation by representatives of organizations. The committee, aware that the report is to be made to representatives of all the agencies with which it deals, has done a comprehensive and careful piece of work; hence there are only minor corrections. Then the committee goes on to point out what seems to be the particular problem. Young adults in the community do not have any particular place to go or things to do recreationally. The husbands are still physically active and eager for the basketball they remember from their high-school days, while the wives feel the need of contacts and cultural opportunities beyond the narrow horizon of household duties. But little children at home to care for and lack of facilities for organized fun leave them nothing but commercial recreation for their good time.

What is to be done? The item of children to be tended is quickly disposed of by church representatives who indicate that the women's organizations working in concert will provide a baby pen where the youngsters may be parked once a week. Doing the work co-operatively and spreading responsibility among several groups makes little work for everybody concerned.

The problem of a recreational program takes more time. High-school representatives wonder if a night a week during the winter might not be designated for these young married men in the use of the gym, but the gym seems to be busy every night in the week now. They agree that these young men have a claim and a need and that they will take it up with the faculty and school board at the high school. As for more general social events, Grange representatives indicate that their hall might be used by the young people from time to time. The county agent's representative chimes in with information that he can secure expert help for them in learning folk games or in planning and producing a play if this is the sort of thing they want to do. Thus various represented agencies commit themselves to carry out the actual program of ministering to the unmet recreational needs of young married adults.

The most important principle revealed in the foregoing is that the council shall never do anything by or for itself. It serves only in a consultative capacity, leaving action for constituent groups. This rule ought never to be broken, for the moment a council develops a program of its own, carried on apart from the agencies of the community, that moment the council itself becomes another agency competing against the rest. To remain a council, it must scrupulously refrain from action, calling upon its constituent elements to carry forward the plans it initiates. Some may feel impatient at this procedure, convinced that they could do faster on their own what moves so slowly when given to others to do. Such an impression is an illusion; the council which attempts things for itself will soon find itself not a council at all but merely an added organization competing with other organizations for community support.

Most councils operate without any treasury, paying whatever costs arise out of the treasuries of the separate groups. Recently a Virginia rural-community council reported a plan whereby it meets the increasingly burdensome appeals for financial help coming to the various agencies of the community from outside organizations. At the beginning of the year the council decides how much the community as a whole ought to contribute to these various outside appeals. This total amount is then prorated among the several constituent organizations of the council, and they pay their assessments into a council treasury; the council makes grants from this treasury to the various organizations coming with appeals, much as a community chest makes grants in a city. In return for this lump sum the appealing agencies agree to make no further solicitation of local organizations, though they may solicit individuals within the community. The plan saves time on the part of organizations canvassing in the community, does not require each community agency to consider each separate appeal as it comes, and guarantees that funds will be expended in terms of total need rather than to the appeals getting their requests in early. Such a development is not essential to the work of an effective community council, but it does indicate a way in which such a council may render added service to the community. This plan has in some cases been expanded to a house-to-house community-fund canvass under the sponsorship of the council.

It is particularly important to note that we have been speaking not of a village council but of a community council. When attempts are made to establish a council, there is always the danger that village interest and the ease with which contacts with villagers are made will lead us into an unwitting failure to secure representatives of the total community. Care must be taken that farm members of village organizations are included as representatives of their organizations and that open-country churches and neighborhood clubs within the community area are invited to send representatives and to be active in council affairs. A council is useful precisely as it is representative. When large classes of citizens are unrepresented, a council program at best can be only paternalistic.

A problem frequently encountered in council organization is that of determining the basis of representation of such groups as churches which have subsidiary agencies within their own structure. Shall the Methodist church have two representatives, and shall there be two more each for the Methodist Sunday school and the Woman's Society of Christian Service? Obviously such a procedure has to stop somewhere, or every member of the Methodist church would be on the community council. Most council constitutions stipulate that no subsidiary organizations shall have representatives; that is, that there be two representatives from the Methodist church and two only. Sometimes representatives at large are chosen, either to allow influential persons not named to the council by any organization to be called upon for service or to secure the viewpoint of a class of persons not apt to be represented among official delegates—youth, for example. Such representation at large is fraught with considerable danger, in that it introduces into council affairs two kinds of delegates—those responsible to and for a specific group and those with no definite group responsibility at all. Since the council can always call in persons not members to give it special information or guidance, there seems to be little real necessity for representatives at large. Some councils stipulate that a youth representative be appointed by each youth-serving organization.

There is always the further danger that a council will be satisfied with its accomplishment when it has prevented duplication of effort within the community and secured such common plans as will prevent conflict over dates and the use of public facilities. These functions are important, but they are not the most important work of the council. That work is to see that the community it serves is made a good and satisfying place for all its people. A properly functioning community council will soon get beyond the stage of adjudicating possible disputes between organizations and will focus upon meeting the unmet needs of all persons within the borders of its area of influence. It will emphasize, in the long run, not what is being done, but what is being left undone; and it will give its efforts over to planning for programs to care for neglected areas of community life. The church is concerned with such a program, because it offers enrichment to the lives of all the people.

15

THE ROLE OF THE CHURCH IN THE COMMUNITY

MOST OF US are familiar with the fact that personality is the product of living in groups. We are potentially human, but we do not develop into human beings outside a human environment. Man is distinguished from other forms of life in particular by the long period of his infancy and his complete helplessness as an infant. We are socially concerned and conditioned persons because from birth life itself depends upon our being cared for by other, more mature human beings. At birth we are equipped only with a mechanism by which we can call our needs to the attention of other human beings. Our first act is a simple cry for the help of those about us. Our lives begin and continue in society or not at all.

The negative side of this fact is underscored by the few cases which have come to light historically in which human infants have been brought up without contact with other, more mature human beings. In every such case the creature resulting from such unhappy treatment has been far less than a human being. It seems abundantly clear that the distinct development of human potentialities depends upon the stimulation of the infant organism by an intimate human environment from its earliest weeks of life.

Human nature in the family

The first group which affects the infant organism is the family. In the family our human nature develops. Mother, father, brothers, sisters, minister to the appetites and needs of the new arrival. His cries are constantly rewarded by their attentions. And these attentions are not mechanically rendered but are accompanied by pettings and cooings and all the endearments in word and action that families use. Soon the endearments become as important an element in the life of the baby as his food and cleanness. Soon he learns that certain conduct on his part shuts off the endearments which he has come to expect and enjoy. Insensibly at first, and then with more and more purpose, he adopts patterns of behavior which maintain and amplify the friendly conduct of others toward himself which he has come to treasure. In conforming to their expectations in order to remain in their good graces, he first begins to sense what or who he is. He is a "good baby," "Mama's darling," "Daddy's little soldier," "Sister's pet." These various titles stand for specific forms of behavior, not always consistent, which gain for him in the family circle that position of appreciation and consideration which he has come to desire as much as he desires food.

What the family actually does is to internalize in the infant its particular definition of what it is to be human. At first there well may be, as we have indicated, inconsistencies between the expectation of one family member and that of another. But these are removed or accommodated in the give and take of family experience. The role of Father's little "toughy" and the role of Mother's "good boy" are harmonized by finding expression, the one in neighborhood play, the other when the family is entertaining guests. Thus by the time the child is old enough for school, he has discovered and developed within his human environment a fundamental core of ideas and ideals as to himself and his relationship to others by which he can conduct himself as a person among persons.

But every pastor is familiar with the limitations and immaturities of a personality which has never related itself to any but family expectations. Here is a sixty-year-old son of a doting and possessive mother who still comes to her to have his tie arranged and his hair combed, who has never been able to emancipate himself from her dominance and achieve an independent life of his own.

Civic nature in the school

Personality requires to be socialized in terms of a wider-than-family loyalty, and this socialization takes place in the school. School here is used in no narrow or formal sense but rather to refer to that complex of agencies which shapes growing personalities outside the family. Besides the school in the classroom sense we include the Boy and Girl Scouts, the 4-H Club, the F.F.A., organized church-school classes, the neighborhood gang. In these groups associated with school life the child becomes something more than "Mama's boy." He becomes a good citizen of his home room, a loyal member of the team, a good scout, one of the gang. His definitions of personality are broadened by the expectations his schoolmates place upon him. He learns to think of himself not simply as a member of a family but as a member of a community. Just as our human nature is developed in the family, so our civic nature or community nature is developed in the school: we learn that our responsibilities and relationships do not end at the threshold of the home but move out into the community of which we are a part.

Divine nature in the church

But personality formed in terms of community standards and loyalties is still immature and incomplete. Indeed, the social evils of our time may be explained in part by the fact that men and women whose personalities have never grown beyond the community level are living economically and politically in a single world. Their world is too big for them. Religion has always sensed and insisted upon a third level of development. Indeed, religion may well be interpreted as man's quest for a fundamental integration of his life, not simply within the family or within the community, but within the universe—the totality of things. "Here we have no continuing city," says the

186

authentic voice of vital religion. "But we look for 'a city which hath foundations, whose builder and maker is God.'" Just as we become human in the family and civic- or community-minded in the school, so in the church we become divine or saved, or sons and daughters of God, or members of his Kingdom. The work of the church is to direct or form personality in terms of cosmic or universal loyalties.

This new level of personality development comes as we learn experientially within the church to relate our lives consciously and explicitly to the life of God. We become God's children, God's servants, and as such find ourselves suddenly related to our brothers in a completely new light. There are three dimensions in this new relationship. First of all, we discover that our true lives are not limited in space, that we are something more than local personalities whose loyalties are exhausted by local persons and groups. We find that our concern for and relationship to other persons scorns national boundaries so that we join hands around the world. Among us as churchmen there is neither German nor Britisher, Japanese nor Russian, white nor black, ally nor enemy, but only brothers and sisters owing a surpassing salvation to Christ and in his Spirit forgiving and treasuring one another.

Again, we discover that our lives are not completely limited in time, that we are not only citizens of this calendar year, but that we are citizens of all ages and all times. The eleventh chapter of Hebrews gives this view its classic expression. Though the chapter is basically a demonstration of the universal necessity and power of faith, it becomes as well a long and inspiring catalogue of those men and women with whom the Christian cannot but feel a basic and present fellowship. And the Christian age has added to that list the names of the martyrs and saints and servants of the church. Paul, Augustine, Francis, Luther, Wesley, Booth, are our fellows as much as the man in the next pew. "And these all, having obtained a good report through faith, received not the promise: God having provided some better thing for us, that they without us should not be made perfect."

The last phrase suggests the third dimension in which the personality-shaping work of the church takes place. We discover not only that our personalities must have a universal reference in space and in time but also that we must have a consciousness of the universal and eternal meaning of our every act. The Christian acts in a world of eternal consequences. He knows that sin has cosmic proportions, that because of man's sin God sent his own Son into the world to suffer and die, that sin is an eternal threat to the good plan of God. And if man, in sinning, effects results which shake the universe to the core, so man in obedience to God, in the fellowship of the saints, carries on activities which last forever. We must repudiate all false distinctions between sacred and secular in the light of the fact that life's every act has eternal repercussions.

Within the rural community there are today many agencies looking beyond the community, even around the world. Their outlook, however, is basically conditioned by the needs and the standards of the community from which they look. They look beyond purely local affairs because their crops must be sold on a world market or their sons must die in a world war. But their motivation and their standard always lie within the local community. They do not have standards which transcend it. The church does have such a community-transcending standard, for the fundamental loyalty of the churchman is beyond space and time. The expectations to which he reacts in all his conduct are not the expectations of his fellows but of his Father. Not that he feels that he is living up to these expectations or has achieved or become perfect; he is fully aware that when we have done all, we are still "unprofitable servants." But his conduct is constantly swayed in great ways and in small by a reference to standards and values in the light of which his community as well as he is judged.

If this be the social role of the church, what of the condition of the actual rural churches which must carry out this role concretely? We can make the following summary statements about our actual rural churches:

1. They are dominantly Christian. According to the United States Census of Religious Bodies for 1936 (the latest such census available) there were only 142 rural synagogues against 3,587 urban. Of Jewish congregations 96.2 per cent were urban, and 99.1 per cent of Jews were urban.

2. Rural churches are dominantly Protestant. Again according to the 1936 Census of Religious Bodies, only 19.4 per cent of Roman Catholics were rural; but 62.1 per cent of Southern Baptists, 86.1 per cent of Mennonites, and 92.2 per cent of the Amish were rural.

3. Rural congregations are small in numbers. Urban churches averaged 541 members in 1936; rural, 143. This is not true, however, of such dominantly rural fellowships as the Mennonites.

4. They share their pastoral leadership with other rural churches, so that two or more churches are served by the same pastor. Occasionally a single church will employ a pastor who supplements the salary paid him by the church by other, nonecclesiastical employment. In either case the individual church secures only a part of the services of a pastor.

5. They reflect the class and status patterns of their communities. This fact has already been discussed in Chapter 12.

6. They are often so located and oriented to population that several congregations compete for the membership and support of a small number of persons in a rural village, while hundreds of persons go neglected without any church service in open-country areas.

The question has been raised by concerned students: Can a social institution as weak and competitive as the rural church exert the unifying influence which we have indicated is its social responsibility? The answer must be that man always appears too weak and witless to carry out God's designs, but that nevertheless we must respond to the divine will as best we can. It is certainly possible for the rural church to fail; what is unthinkable is that it should cease to try. Our faith is that when we obey God, his power enables us to effect what by ourselves seems quite beyond us. We shall examine in the remainder of the chapter functions which these actual weak rural churches must pursue in living out their social responsibilities.

The church as co-operator

The first function of the church in the rural community is to serve as the champion of co-operation. This follows from the social function of the church. If the church is to point personality to standards and expectations which transcend the community, then it must develop attitudes of co-operation within the community. To preach world fellowship on the one hand at the same time that we deny or impede human co-operation in our own specific community on the other is to doom our message to sterility and ineffectuality. The church must preach co-operation, not because it is efficient or because it will save money and energy, but because it is Christian. We are to work together, offering every assistance to one another, because Christ in his life and death sought to bridge the gaps separating man and God and man and man. This function of the church is fundamental and primary. When we fail to fulfill it, we are in grave danger of ceasing to be a church at all.

The church must co-operate with other churches in the community first of all. Nothing weakens and dilutes our message in the community more than tne example of churches which do not work together. Co-operation among churches is always possible, though the area of possible co-operation is much larger in the case of certain denominations than others. Several methods have been worked out for forwarding this unification, and we shall discuss them as possible implementations of our ideal.

Exchange of rights

The first possibility open—one useful only in situations where there are two churches of similar denominations in two communities—is the method of exchange of rights. The Methodist Church and the Evangelical Church have congregations in both Independence and Arcadia. The Methodist pastor lives in Independence, and as he is driving to Arcadia every Sunday to hold church there, he meets on the journey the Evangelical pastor on his way from his parsonage in Arcadia to hold services in Independence. Both pastors are spreading themselves over two communities and ministering to weak congregations in both. The Methodist denomination, strong in Independence, offers to exchange its church in Arcadia for the Evangelical church in Independence; the arrangements are perfected, and now each community has a pastor to itself, and each pastor has a self-sufficient church. The situations in which this can be done are, of course, distinctly limited, but where such a plan can be carried out, it is ideal.

Federation

A second plan—this one more generally applicable—is that of church federation. It is often used in village situations where there exist two or more churches of equal strength. These churches agree to maintain their denominational affiliations intact but to act, in local affairs, as a single congregation. This means that they call one pastor, unite in common worship, and amalgamate Sunday schools, women's organizations, brotherhoods, and youth associations. People still belong to the Methodist or Baptist or Congregational Christian church as the case may be; assessments are still paid, according to agreement, to the several denominational bodies; but in the local community there is a single church program and a united church leadership. Difficulties sometimes center in the matter of securing pastoral leadership, since often the agreement provides that a pastor shall be called from each of the federated denominations in rotation. Such a plan makes many a man unwilling to accept a call or appointment to a federated church, because he knows that he will not be succeeded by a pastor from his own denomination. Since he will not be making an opening for another pastor of his denomination, there may be no opening for him. If the number of federated churches increases, however, this will not prove a difficulty, since shifts among federated-church pastors will be taking place more frequently with the greater number of churches.

Larger parish

A third type of co-operation is the larger parish. A larger parish may be defined as one in which there is unification of all the religious work in a community area under a single pastoral staff. A community area is determined, and then all churches within that area, village and open country, are asked to join in a working agreement setting up a larger-parish council. This council calls a pastor to direct the parish, and he in turn sets up a staff of persons to work with him. On this staff there may be, in addition to the chief pastor, a women's worker and a youth worker. These two with the pastor will preach and conduct worship in the various co-operating churches; but they will *all* serve *all* the churches. Furthermore, they will bring together the work of the churches at points where unity will strengthen the religious program. Youth work will be unified, for example, so that there will not be half a dozen small youth groups but one large group with an ambitious program, broken down for work purposes into neighborhood divisions.

An example will make the program clear. Here in a community area of sixty-seven square miles about a village of eight hundred people are a total of nine evangelical churches. A Roman Catholic church in the village center must be left out of our planning for the obvious reason of its denominational polity. The nine churches which we expect to weld into a larger parish are located four in the village and five in the surrounding countryside. They now partially employ a total of seven pastors: two of the village churches have resident pastors of their own; one other village church is served by a pastor coming in from the county-seat town twenty miles away; the fourth village church is related to one of the country churches in the same community in employing a pastor; two of the open-country churches are tied in with a third church in an adjoining community area in a single circuit served by a common pastor; the other two open-country churches are each related to other out-side churches in securing pastoral service. Thus only three of the seven pastors serving churches within the community are exclusively related to this community. All salaries are low, the best-paid man being one of the village pastors who receives his parsonage and $2,800 a year; yet the total amount expended for pastoral leadership by the community is $11,000, excluding the rental value of four parsonages furnished. Of the pastors serving within the area, only one has met the educational requirements set up for the ministry by his denominations—namely, both a college and a seminary degree. Denominations represented are Methodist, Presbyterian, and Congregational Christian.

These churches decide that they can serve their people and their community in a more Christian fashion if they consolidate their resources and act as a unit. They agree to come together in employing their pastoral leadership and in developing their local program; each church is to remain a separate organization with responsibility and loyalty to its particular denomination. They set up a council, constituted of an equal number of representatives from each church, and this council elects certain committees, among which is a committee on pastoral relationships. The council instructs this committee to call a pastor and to assist him in setting up a staff, with the understanding that, insofar as good leadership is available, the persons constituting the staff shall represent each of the denominations participating.

The committee locates and secures a well-trained and experienced pastor at a salary of $4,000 a year and parsonage. His suggestion, after surveying the community, is that a junior pastor be employed at a salary of $3,000 a year and parsonage and that a woman director of religious education be employed at $2,400 and lodging. Thus for $9,400 a year the staff of the larger parish is secured—three people to give their full and undivided time to that particular community. The $1,600 remaining from the total amount paid to former pastors is put into a transportation account on which staff members draw at so much per mile for their parish duties. Under former arrangements only the two village churches with full-time pastors had worship services every Sunday. Now with three pastors among nine churches it is possible for each church so to be served if it wishes. As a matter of fact, the congregations prefer to maintain the old schedule pretty much unaltered but to have each Sunday evening a parish-wide worship service in one of the churches, with the choir of another church furnishing music and with special dramatic programs from time to time.

The religious-education program of the churches is improved; teachers now know that they have a sympathetic expert in education on their own staff to whom they can go at any time with particular problems. The nine churches come together each winter for a leadership-training school, and the old desultory teachers' meetings of the separate Sunday schools are replaced with monthly teachers' meetings for the whole parish, in which there is the stimulation and inspiration of interaction with other teachers from all over the community. Youth work is integrated and a program developed which catches the imagination and challenges the participation and leadership of even the most intelligent and active young people.

All these advantages are secured at no added cost to the constituent churches but at exactly the same figure they originally paid their seven part-time pastors. Treasurers are amazed to discover, however, that funds are now much easier to secure. People outside the churches know the pastors by sight; they meet them every day on street or country road; they appreciate what religion is now doing, not just for church members, but for all the community. And the churches now make a united appeal and canvass; no longer can anyone pass one set of canvassers off with the story that his interest is in another church, for each set of canvassers represents the churches as a whole. A united approach to the community makes a more efficient use of the resources of the community, so that at the end of two years there are funds to add another member to the staff if this proves desirable.

Further, through the larger parish the religious forces of the community have secured a parity of influence with other forces. Just as the superintendent of schools speaks for all the schools of the community, so the chief pastor of the parish speaks for all the churches of the community. When the religious emphasis in community life has a single authoritative spokesman, it is much more apt to be heard in community affairs. Insensibly but vitally, religion takes hold of community life, setting higher standards and creating sensitivities which did not exist before. And all of this is accomplished without the destruction of any church organization or the harming of the interest of any denomination. When you consider the values to be had, it is amazing that we do not make a more frequent use of this method.

Group ministry

A final technique for working together in churches is the group ministry. This aims at the same results as does the larger parish but begins with the ministry rather than with the organization. It is the plan whereby ministers within a community area agree to work together as a unit or team. It may be as simple as an agreement to carry on their religious-education programs according to a concerted plan and with consultation and cooperation in such matters as teacher recruitment and training; it may be as complete as the pooling of salaries and the sharing of ministerial obligations and responsibilities within individual parishes.

The idea of a group ministry has grown out of our consciousness that the modern rural community demands a variety of talent and training in its ministry which one man can scarcely supply. A variety of needs requires a teamwork in service. So men of diverse training and ability come together in a common effort to serve their respective parishes within the community and form what amount to a religious co-operative. They bring to the problems and struggles of each church not simply the strength, consecration, and talent of one man but the combined strength and abilities of the group. A church regarded by all denominational officials as hopeless was served by a member of such a ministry; at the end of his first year the church for the first time in its history reported all bills paid and a treasury balance. A financial plan worked out in the sessions of the group ministry had been applied by this pastor thoughtfully and conscientiously, and the result was a self-evident vindication of the group approach.

Such an approach to ministerial service has much to offer to the individual pastor. From the group he constantly receives criticism through which his weaknesses are made apparent and corrected, thus avoiding the paralyzing self-satisfaction and smugness which grow out of constant and well-meant lay appreciation. On the other hand, his strong points are appreciated by persons whose understanding is objective, and he is thereby encouraged to develop his basic capabilities as he might not were he serving alone. Within the group he develops a strong sense of fellowship and is given that opportunity for expressing personal affection so often denied ministers. Economically and professionally the group provides him with security, for there is always a brother minister ready to take over his responsibilities if sickness or emergency prevents his meeting them. And the group continually sets for the participating minister a standard for his administration of his own church or churches.

In the long run, the larger parish and group ministry aim at the same result. The larger parish approaches this end from the point of view of the organization of the churches themselves; the group ministry makes its approach from the point of view of pastoral leadership. Both plans deserve the most careful scrutiny and consideration by the rural pastor and by general church leaders who desire to bring the church to the service of the community in which it has its home.

As champion of co-operation, the church has responsibility for initiating and supporting such community movements of co-operation as are discussed in Chapter 14. But churches teach co-operation to the community by their own example of inter-church co-operation.

The church as community conscience

A second role of the church is to be the moral conscience of the community. It is here perhaps that most pastors are conscious of their responsibility to the community and that most laymen are eager for the church to speak and act. Too often our picture of the action of a moral conscience is limited and one-sided. We think that conscience exists but to condemn. As a matter of fact, conscience roots in and acts from a sense of values. It has as much the duty to praise as to censure, and its sense of the unique and eternal value of human beings leads it to censure only with extreme sorrow. Any criticisms of community activities which carry in them a note of smugness, of self-righteousness, or of rejoicing in the sufferings of the wicked are not motivated by a Christian conscience but by human pride in our own standards and achievements.

The church must praise the good in its community, and the pastor may well take the lead in this matter. Let him be the one to point the finger of appreciation at the faithful school-teacher whose influence is so effective for good among the boys of the community. Let him be the one to assess the manliness that develops out of the farm projects of the Future Farmers of America under the leadership of the high-school vocational-agriculture teacher. Let him be the one to call a fitting attention to the real but unostentatious service rendered the community by the unpaid librarian. Let his people learn appreciation not only without but within the church from him.

There are agencies and practices in the community which the church must condemn and seek to eliminate. Let such condemnation always be given in a spirit of humility and sorrow. If evils exist in our community, we are partly at fault. Evil could not come if it did not find a home among us—a home we create for it, willingly or unwillingly. Let us, moreover, always be sure of our facts. Many a righteous cause has been defeated because it sought support in terms that were proved invalid by the facts. It is always a temptation to paint the evil as dramatically bad as we can. Beware an overstatement which will eventually boomerang upon our cause. Beware also any bitterness in condemnation. There is no excuse anywhere in the life or words of Jesus for bitterness in our treatment of either his enemies or ours.

Finally, the moral conscience of the community not only must praise the good and condemn the evil but also must develop a sense for the unmet needs of the community. Many evil agencies exist within a community, not because they are evil, but because of the good they do. The church must sense human need and see that that need is met somewhere. During a no-license campaign in a rural village, a member of the church, who had been praying much about the matter, came to her pastor and said: "I notice that many of the patrons of the bar-room are old men in town, men who have no other place to go for warmth and company. They go into the tavern not particularly to drink but to meet other old men and to break their loneliness. This is a good service which the saloons are rendering to our community, and, in my opinion, the church must open social rooms for these older men in town if we succeed in closing the bars." Here was a church member who realized that a moral conscience involves responsibilities for the real needs of men and women.

The church as supplement

This leads us to a third role which the church must assume in the community: it must be a supplemental agency. We have already pointed out that the church has only one unique role—the maturing of personality through reference to God as our ultimate loyalty. This is the only thing which the church must do, and it does this fundamentally as it conducts worship before God. But there are any number of things which the church may do; indeed, it ought to undertake anything which needs to be done in the community and which no other agency is prepared to undertake.

Whenever the church, in its search for unmet needs, finds a task which no other agency is equipped to meet, then the church ought to undertake that task. This is an accepted principle in the mission field. The missionary opens a hospital, organizes a school, begins a program of public works, establishes new agricultural practices. Whatever needs doing, he, as representative of the church, does. The same principle has held with the church historically; churchmen developed the hotel, the hospital, the university. These agencies have become self-sustaining, and the church gladly frees itself of them and goes on to do the new tasks that meet today's needs.

One of the special groups with great need in the rural community today is made up of those sixty-five years of age and older. These people, making up as much as a third of the population in some rural villages, have little to do and much time to do it. Many rural churches ought to start an "age program" for their communities similar to the youth programs we have developed. Already the Methodist denomination, through its Board of Education, is sponsoring summer camps for people over sixty-five. These camps are to have a program of classes, discussion, and recreation such as we are accustomed to in youth institutes, except that the topics and methods used will be graded to the greater maturity of the persons involved. The church has a supplemental function in its community.

A small rural church in northern Illinois noted that the high-school pupils of the town had a splendid recreational program provided for them, while the grade-school pupils had none. "Why should we," they asked, "compete with the high school by providing recreation for our high-school young people when our grade-school boys and girls are suffering from neglect?" The church grounds adjoined those of the grade school; and the men of the church, directed by their pastor, arranged a playground with suitable equipment on church property for grade-school youth. During recesses and on Saturdays the pastor, teachers, and other church leaders offered supervision and directed play for the grade-schoolers. Here again the church was fulfilling its supplementary function.

The church as experimenter

A fourth role of the church is experimental. In most communities it is the only agency which can afford to experiment, for experimentation carries with it the possibility of failure. The school superintendent must succeed or he is asked to move; the banker or grocer must succeed or lose his business; but the church as an institution immediately responsible to its people can afford to fail in some detail of its program and learn thereby. A pastor might well take as a standard for a church in sound condition to carry on at least one experimental activity each year—one program in which we test out some new approach to our work. This the church in its totality has done in the past. Many of the new departures in education have been pioneered in religious education because the church experimented in ways the public schools dared not.

In connection with the Lord's Acre projects churches have experimented with and proved for their communities new types or strains of seed. In connection with church buildings and property, construction methods and materials of an experimental nature have been developed and proved. On occasion, though in this case more abroad than at home, the church on its own farmlands has pioneered new methods of agriculture and new crops to the ultimate benefit of the whole countryside. One pastor even put tithing on an experimental basis by getting a large number of his families to tithe through Lent. So happy were they with the experience that the church raised its total budget for the ensuing year by pledges without having to make recourse to church suppers or entertainments or any other type of commercial activity.

The church training community leaders

A fifth role of the church lies in training leaders for positions of community responsibility. Often a pastor says in complaint: "I had young John Cobb in my teacher-training class two years ago, and he was a most promising find for my Sunday school, but I've lost him now. He's serving as president of the Farm Bureau." Such a statement indicates how institution-centered, rather than gospel-centered, we are. We ought to rejoice when a young man or woman we have trained is honored by elevation to a position of community leadership, for it means that the standards we have set as to method and goal of leadership are having an effect far beyond the limits of our own organization. Such leaders in action in nonchurch settings are not lost to us so long as they maintain the ideals they caught from us. Indeed, the more we can put Christian leaders at the head of secular organizations, the more our American public life will present an opportunity for expressing Christian convictions in public policy.

There is some evidence that the church is sensing its responsibility at this point. Calvin Schnucker as program director for the Iowa Christian Rural Fellowship made a study of Iowa rural youth-organization leaders in 1941. Of the officers of such organizations 82 per cent were church members in thirteen denominations, 79 per cent attended church regularly, and 82 per cent supported the church financially. In contrast, only 52 per cent of the nonofficer members of such organizations participated in church programs. Certainly the leaders of the organizations were more influenced by the church than the rank and file of the same groups. A Wisconsin study of my own, however, reveals certain disturbing elements. Pastors with the aid of a rating sheet were asked to list the marks of an effective Christian according to the teaching of their particular denomination. When these marks were established, the pastor was then asked to give the names of five families in his church who measured up acceptably on all the criteria. Thus was built up a list of sixty-one families within a small area who, according to their spiritual leaders, were the most effectively evangelized persons of the community. I then visited the county agent, county superintendent of schools, and the home-demonstration agent and asked them to list the families in the same area on whom they would call for leadership in community enterprises. They listed thirty-eight different families. Only five of the thirty-eight listed by the secular officials appeared on the list of "best Christians" furnished by the pastors. That a list of thirty-eight community leaders and a list of sixty-one most effective Christians would contain only five names in common indicates that Christians with whom the professional leaders of the various denominations are most pleased are not recognized as responsible leaders in the general life of their communities.

There is no necessary contradiction between the two studies. The Iowa study indicates that leaders, more than followers, in general community affairs attend church; the Wisconsin study indicates that those with whom the church is most successful are not motivated to community leadership. In other words, the churches seem to be sending out something less than their best to represent them in the leadership of the secular life of the community. None of us can be very happy about such a situation. All of us can strive to remedy it by building within ourselves and among our people a sense of Christian responsibility for community leadership.

The church—colony of the Kingdom

Dr. Aaron H. Rapking has pointed out to me that the church in the rural community has a unique role as representing the kingdom of God. Not that the church is God's kingdom in any perfect or final sense, but that the ideals of the Kingdom are made real in the local community only through the life of the church. In the group life of Christian people secular agencies of the community discern the standards and principles of social conduct which should guide them. The secular agencies should be able to say as they look at Christians in the fellowship of the church: "See how they love one another."

This means that the internal affairs of the church play an important role in the total life of the community. The spirit in which the official board settles the business affairs of the parish, the attitude with which the trustees of the church deal with businessmen in town, are important influences for or against God's kingdom. High standards of personal conduct coupled with an outgoing helpfulness to all in need preach an eloquent gospel. The practice of the church, whether for good or for ill, soon becomes the standard of the community. We have abundant evidence that this is true whenever the church fails to live up to her own high standard. We have little doubt that this will be true when the church trusts the gospel in carrying on her affairs within the community.

In thus standing as a concrete example of God's kingdom the church helps to integrate the life of the community in a vital sense. Other agencies and institutions, won by the practice of the church to the way of the Master of the church, begin to see their task and interpret their programs in terms of unselfish and un-self-regarding co-operation. Their approximation in secular life of the ideal disclosed to them in the church results in a lessening of tensions and a cessation of conflicts. Thus, without any dictatorial force, but through the pull of an ideal, community activities begin to assume a unified pattern and work to a single end. With what power this process moves can best be seen in the history of such colonizing sects as the Mennonites or the Mormons. Where the church in practice lives out its own gospel, whatever that gospel may be, it profoundly shapes and unifies the life of the entire community.

The church—sanctuary

Finally, the church should be a sanctuary for all within the community. This thought is as old as religion. It appears again and again in the Old Testament in the provision of cities of refuge or in the protection even a wrongdoer might claim before the altar. Every society needs an institution to which a man can appeal and "no questions asked." Without such an institution available to their needs men grow desperate and then quite mad. When a man finds every hand against him, something within his personality breaks, and he becomes a wild animal, setting himself against the human world.

This does not mean that the pastor or church should shelter the criminal or help him to escape the penalty of his folly. It means rather that every criminal, as every other man, should have the right to appeal, the right to a listening ear and an understanding spirit, the right to such counsel as will set him again in the paths of peace. Unless such a shelter is available to him, he turns into a beast fighting all society ranged against him. Society leaves him no alternative but to fight and to kill, because it presents him with no shelter where he can talk of his difficulties with an understanding, uncondemning friend.

Most of the persons who need sanctuary are not criminals. They are the drunkard, the ne'er-do-well, the immoral woman, the down-at-the-heels migrant. And the minister as representative of the church must offer asylum to them all. His must be the door in every village where a man may knock and not turn away empty-handed. Some will argue that thus the pastor is victimized and dishonest men confirmed in their evil ways. The average rural pastor has so little of this world's wealth that he could scarcely with all of it confirm any man in an evil way. So long as he limits his aid to the provision of that shelter, food, and counsel which every wayfarer needs, he cannot but be an instrument through whom Christ extends the cup of cold water.

There is a risk of misunderstanding here. I do not mean that the pastor should ever allow his zeal in philanthropy to overcome his sense of justice. Too often Christian people have permitted their show of benevolence to blind them to social inequities from which they were obtaining marked material benefits. What I have said already about the church as moral conscience should indicate that the church must be the champion of basic righteousness in economic as in other relationships within the community. But perfect justice when it comes will not do away with the need for grace and sanctuary, and these the church must administer to all. Every pastor should establish his parsonage home as one place in the community where all men are always welcome. Thus he will set an example of basic benevolence which will permeate the life of the whole community.

Across the mountains and prairies of our great country are scattered thousands of little churches. They are, in a real sense, the hope of their world. Without them life grows coarse, family love suffers and decays, education becomes a device for personal aggrandizement, farming is merely a gambler's game. When they are strong, men are strong in the elemental qualities of honesty, fairness, tolerance, and pity. As we tend them, we fulfill the God-given task of spreading scriptural holiness throughout the land.

NOTES

Volumes and bulletins here mentioned are listed in the Bibliography. An excellent bibliographical statement is Burchfield, *Our Rural Communities*. These notes and references should serve to introduce the student to the general literature in the field of rural church and community relationships.

1. *WHAT DO WE MEAN BY "RURAL"?*

For a development of some of the points raised in this chapter the student should turn to Kolb and Brunner, *A Study of Rural Society,* chap. 1. Loomis and Beegle in *Rural Social Systems* discuss rural-urban differentiation from a more theoretical point of view. The theory behind the typological approach is ably discussed in the Wiese-Becker text, *Systematic Sociology,* in a note on sacred and secular societies, pp. 222 ff.

2. *THE FRAMEWORK OF RURAL SOCIETY*

The structure of rural society is analyzed in all rural-sociology texts. Besides the Kolb and Brunner text already mentioned (chaps. 2-5), an excellent treatment may be found in Sims, *Elements of Rural Sociology,* Part II. Sanderson, *Rural Sociology and Rural Social Organization,* chaps. 10-14, gives another excellent development of the same material.

It has been found convenient to measure fertility in any population group by what is known as a fertility ratio. This ratio is the number of children under five years of age per one thousand women fifteen through forty-four. Women fifteen through forty-four represent the potential fertility of any population. Few children are born to mothers below the age of fifteen or above the age of forty-five. All women, married or unmarried, within these age limits represent that portion of the population capable of giving birth to children. The number of children under five years of age gives the actual realized fertility of these women. To take the number under five rather than the number born is a better measure because it

207

takes into account not only babies born but babies living. A high infant-mortality rate may counteract the effect of a high birth rate.

Walter L. Slocum and Herman M. Case of the State College of Washington discuss the question of the general existence of neighborhoods in rural America in an article entitled "Are Neighborhoods Meaningful Social Groups?" in *Rural Sociology*, Vol. XVIII, No. 1, for March, 1953.

3. FITTING THE CHURCH TO ITS COMMUNITY

Here the most complete material is found in Stotts, *The Church Inventory Handbook*. There are also helpful suggestions in Sanders, *Making Good Communities Better*.

4. LAND: TOO LITTLE OR TOO MUCH

General background for chapters 4 through 7 is found in Benedict, *Farm Policies of the United States, 1790-1950*. Read Ely and Wehrwein, *Land Economics*, chaps. 3, 6, 7. The discussion in Chapters IV-VI of this book follows that of Ely and Wehrwein very closely.

5. LAND: BREAD AND BUTTER

For further analysis note Ely and Wehrwein, *Land Economics*, chap. 2; *Soils and Men* (Yearbook of Agriculture, 1938); *Farmers in a Changing World* (Yearbook of Agriculture, 1940); Osborn, *Our Plundered Planet*; Vogt, *Road to Survival*.

6. LAND: YOURS AND MINE

Further references are available in Ely and Wehrwein, *Land Economics*, chap. 4; and the following reports of the Farm Foundation: *The Church and Land Tenure; The People, the Land, and the Church in the Rural West*. See also Ackerman and Harris, *Family Farm Policy*. Eaton, *Exploring Tomorrow's Agriculture*, gives a suggestive analysis of co-operative farming. Felker, *The Apprentice Farmer*, describes the experiment of the Goodyear Tire and Rubber Company in establishing young families on land of their own.

7. IN UNION STRENGTH

Taylor, *The Farmers' Movement*, is a key volume. Lindstrom, *Farmers' and Rural Organizations*, is most comprehensive. Study also *Farmers in a Changing World*, Parts I, IV; Coleman, *Men and Coal*; McCune, *The Farm Bloc*; Gardner, *The Grange, Friend of the Farmer, 1867-1941*; Kile, *The Farm Bureau Through Three Decades*.

8. *RURAL TRADE*

General discussions of rural trade and trading centers are available in Gee, *The Social Economics of Agriculture,* chap. 24, and Kolb and Brunner, *A Study of Rural Society,* chap. 9. *The Report of the Inquiry on Co-operative Enterprise in Europe, 1937,* contains much important data. Landis, *Bethlehem and Rochdale,* gives a short summary of the relationship of the church and religion to the co-operative movement.

9. *THE RURAL SCHOOL*

All rural-sociology texts contain valuable and pointed treatment of the possibilities and problems of rural education. Kolb and Brunner, *A Study of Rural Society,* chaps. 18, 19, offers an excellent summary. The student ought also to be familiar with material in such pamphlets as *Expenditures for Education at the Mid-Century,* and *Education in Rural and City School Systems.*

10. *OTHER EDUCATIONAL AGENCIES AND PROGRAMS*

Smith and Wilson, *The Agricultural Extension System of the United States,* is an excellent older summary. The student should also refer to Brunner and Yang, *Rural America and the Extension Service.* The whole land-use planning program is analyzed sympathetically in the Bureau of Agricultural Economics bulletin, *Land-Use Planning Under Way.*

11. *RURAL WELFARE*

There are two key volumes here: Landis, *Rural Welfare Services,* and Mott and Roemer, *Rural Health and Medical Care.* See also Schultz, *Agriculture in an Unstable Economy.*

12. *THE SOCIAL-CLASS SYSTEM*

The key volume here is Warner, Meeker, and Eells, *Social Class in America.* See also West, *Plainville, U. S. A.;* Warner, *Democracy in Jonesville;* Havighurst and Taba, *Adolescent Character and Personality;* Dollard, *Caste and Class in a Southern Town;* Hollingshead, *Elmtown's Youth.*

13. *THE COMMUNITY—AN OPPORTUNITY FOR THE CHURCH*

A good general book is Sanders, *Making Good Communities Better;* Baker Brownell has a suggestive point of view in *The Human Community.* For an older book see Sanderson and Polson, *Rural Community Organization.* Seifert, *The Church in Community Action,* has excellent material on the management of conflict.

14. *COMMUNITY ORGANIZATION*

The books listed above under Chapter XIII will help here. See also *The Small Community* by Morgan.

15. *THE ROLE OF THE CHURCH IN THE COMMUNITY*

The view regarding the development of personality discussed here depends upon the theories of Charles H. Cooley and G. H. Mead. A good discussion of the effect of isolation upon personality development is given in Cavan, *The Family*, pp. 212 ff. A general treatment of this point of view is presented in Becker and Hill, *Family, Marriage, and Parenthood*, chap. 7, and in Barnes and Becker, *Contemporary Social Theory*, pp. 337 ff. For an effective discussion from a medical point of view see Ribble, *The Rights of Infants*.

A helpful general point of view will be found in Seifert, *The Church in Community Action*. Richardson in *Dark Glory* gives a summary statement as to the church among Negroes in the rural South. Schnucker, *How to Plan the Rural Church Program,* is a modern treatment.

BIBLIOGRAPHY

Books

Ackerman, Joseph, and Harris, Marshall, eds. *Family Farm Policy*. Chicago: University of Chicago Press, 1946.

Barnes, Harry Elmer; Becker, Howard; and Becker, Frances; eds. *Contemporary Social Theory*. New York: D. Appleton-Century Co., 1940.

Becker, Howard. *Systematic Sociology on the Basis of the* Beziehungslehre *and* Gebildelehre *of Leopold von Wiese*. New York: John Wiley & Sons, 1932.

Becker, Howard, and Hill, Reuben. *Family, Marriage, and Parenthood*. Boston: D. C. Heath & Co., 1955.

Benedict, Murray R. *Farm Policies of the United States, 1790-1950*. New York: The Twentieth Century Fund, 1953.

Bowen, Genevieve. *Living and Learning in a Rural School*. New York: The Macmillan Co., 1944.

Brownell, Baker. *The Human Community*. New York: Harper & Bros., 1950.

Brunner, Edmund deS. *The Larger Parish, A Movement or an Enthusiasm?* New York: Institute of Social and Religious Research, 1934.

———. *Surveying Your Community*. New York: George H. Doran Co., 1925.

Brunner, Edmund deS., and Yang, E. Hsin Pao. *Rural America and the Extension Service*. New York: Board of Publication, Teachers' College, Columbia University, 1949.

Burchfield, Laverne. *Our Rural Communities*. Chicago: Public Administration Service, 1947.

Cavan, Ruth Shonle. *The Family*. New York: Thomas Y. Crowell Co., 1944.

Coleman, McAlister. *Men and Coal*. New York: Farrar & Rinehart, 1943.

Dollard, John. *Caste and Class in a Southern Town*. 2nd ed. New York: Harper & Bros., 1949.

Eaton, Joseph W. *Exploring Tomorrow's Agriculture*. New York: Harper & Bros., 1943.

Ely, Richard T., and Wehrwein, George S. *Land Economics.* New York: The Macmillan Co., 1940.

Gardner, Charles M. *The Grange, Friend of the Farmer, 1867-1947.* New York: J. J. Little & Ives Co., 1949.

Gee, Wilson. *The Social Economics of Agriculture.* 3rd ed. New York: The Macmillan Co., 1954.

Havighurst, Robert J., and Taba, Hilda. *Adolescent Character and Personality.* New York: John Wiley & Sons, Inc., 1949.

Hollingshead, August B. *Elmtown's Youth.* New York: John Wiley & Sons, Inc., 1949.

Kile, O. M. *The Farm Bureau Through Three Decades.* Baltimore, Md.: The Waverly Press, 1948.

Kolb, J. H., and Brunner, Edmund deS. *A Study of Rural Society.* 4th ed. Boston: Houghton Mifflin Co., 1952.

Kress, Andrew J., ed. *Introduction to the Co-operative Movement.* New York: Harper & Bros., 1941.

Landis, Benson Y. *Rural Welfare Services.* New York: Columbia University Press, 1949.

Lindstrom, David Edgar. *American Farmers' and Rural Organizations.* Urbana, Ill.: The Garrard Press, 1948.

Loomis, Charles P., and Beegle, J. Allan. *Rural Social Systems.* New York: Prentice-Hall, Inc., 1950.

McCune, Wesley. *The Farm Bloc.* Garden City: Doubleday, Doran & Co., 1943.

Morgan, Arthur E. *The Small Community.* New York: Harper & Bros., 1942.

Morse, H. N., and Brunner, Edmund deS. *The Town and Country Church in the United States.* New York: George H. Doran Co., 1923.

Mott, Frederick D., and Roemer, Milton I. *Rural Health and Medical Care.* New York: McGraw-Hill Book Co., Inc., 1948.

Myers, A. J. W., and Sundt, Edwin E. *The Country Church As It Is.* New York: Fleming H. Revell Co., 1930.

Osborn, Fairfield, *Our Plundered Planet.* Boston: Little, Brown & Co., 1948.

Ribble, Margaret. *The Rights of Infants.* New York: Columbia University Press, 1943.

Richardson, Harry V. B. *Dark Glory.* New York: Friendship Press, 1947.

Sanders, Irwin T. *Making Good Communities Better.* Lexington, Ky.: University of Kentucky Press, 1950.

Sanderson, Dwight. *Rural Sociology and Rural Social Organization.* New York: John Wiley & Sons, 1942.

Sanderson, Dwight, and Polson, Robert A. *Rural Community Organization.*
New York: John Wiley & Sons, 1939.

Schnucker, Calvin. *How to Plan the Rural Church Program.* Philadelphia:
Westminster Press, 1954.

Schultz, Theodore W. *Agriculture in an Unstable Economy.* New York:
McGraw-Hill Book Co., Inc., 1945.

Seifert, Harvey. *The Church in Community Action.* New York and Nashville: Abingdon Press, 1952.

Sims, Newell LeRoy. *Elements of Rural Sociology.* New York: Thomas Y.
Crowell Co., 1940.

Smith, C. B., and Wilson, M. C. *The Agricultural Extension System of the
United States.* New York: John Wiley & Sons, 1930.

Sorokin, P. A., and Zimmerman, Carle C. *Principles of Rural-Urban
Sociology.* New York: Henry Holt & Co., 1929.

Stotts, Herbert E. *The Church Inventory Handbook.* Denver: Wesley Press,
1952.

Taylor, Carl C. *The Farmers' Movement, 1620-1920.* New York: American Book Co., 1953.

True, A. C. *History of Agricultural Extension Work in the United States.*
Washington: U. S. Department of Agriculture, 1928.

U. S. Department of Agriculture. *Farmers in a Changing World.* 1940.
Washington: Government Printing Office, 1940.

U. S. Department of Agriculture. *Soils and Men.* 1938. Washington: Government Printing Office, 1938.

Vogt, William. *Road to Survival.* New York: William Sloane Associates,
Inc., 1948.

Warner, W. Lloyd, and others. *Democracy in Jonesville.* New York: Harper
& Bros., 1949.

Warner, W. Lloyd; Meeker, Marchia; and Eells, Kenneth. *Social Class in
America.* Chicago: Science Research Associates, 1949.

West, James. *Plainville, U. S. A.* New York: Columbia University Press,
1945.

Bulletins and Pamphlets

Alexander, Frank D., and Nelson, Lowry. *Rural Social Organization, Good-
hue County.* Agricultural Experiment Station, University of Minnesota,
1949.

Bureau of Agricultural Economics. *Land-Use Planning Under Way.* Washington: U. S. Department of Agriculture, July, 1940.

The Church and Land Tenure. Mimeographed. Farm Foundation, 600
S. Michigan Ave., Chicago, Ill., 1940.

The Church in Urban Life, A Fact Book. Methodist Board of Missions, 150
Fifth Avenue, New York 11, N. Y., 1954.

Day, LeRoy J. *What Makes a Church Vital?* A Study of Baptist Rural Churches in the Walworth and Northwestern Associations of Wisconsin. Madison, Wis.: University of Wisconsin College of Agriculture, 1944.

Douglass, H. Paul. *United Local Churches: An Interpretation Illustrated by Case Studies.* New York: Federal Council of the Churches of Christ.

Ensminger, Douglas, and Page, John S. *A Study of Churches of Culpeper County, Virginia.* Culpeper Land-Use Planning Committee and Bureau of Agricultural Economics, July, 1940.

Farm Tenancy. Report of the President's Committee. Washington: Government Printing Office, 1937.

Felker, James. *The Apprentice Farmer.* Akron, Ohio: Goodyear Tire & Rubber Co., 1944.

Felton, Ralph A. *Local Church Co-operation in Rural Communities.* New York: Home Missions Council, 297 Fourth Avenue, New York.

Folson, Josiah C. *Agricultural Labor in the United States, 1943-52.* Washington: U. S. Department of Agriculture, 1954.

Friends of the Soil. Mimeographed statement by Eugene Smathers, chairman, Big Lick, Tennessee, and Howard Kester, executive secretary, Black Mountain, N. C.

Galpin, C. J. *The Country Church, An Economic and Social Force.* Madison, Wis.: Agricultural Experiment Station, University of Wisconsin, January, 1917. Bulletin 278.

Goldsmith, Walter R. *Small Business and the Community.* Senate Committee Print, No. 13. Washington: U. S. Government Printing Office, 1946.

Grigsby, S. Earl, and Hoffsommer, Harold. *Rural Social Organization of Frederick County, Maryland.* College Park, Maryland: The University of Maryland Agricultural Experiment Station, March, 1949. Bulletin No. A 51.

Herlihy, Lester B. *Statistics of City School Systems.* Federal Security Agency, 1953.

Hoosier Churches. A Study of the Rural Congregational Christian Churches of Indiana. New York: Board of Home Missions, Congregational Christian Churches, 1943.

Hutchins, Clayton D., and Munse, Albert R. *Expenditures for Education at the Mid-Century.* U. S. Department of Health, Education, and Welfare, 1953.

Jehlik, Paul J., and Wakeley, Ray E. *Rural Organization in Process.* A Case Study of Hamilton County, Iowa. Ames, Iowa: Agricultural Experiment Station, Iowa State College of Agriculture and Mechanic Arts, September, 1949. Research Bulletin 365.

Kaufman, Harold F. *Prestige Classes in a New York Rural Community.*

Ithaca, New York: Cornell University, Agricultural Experiment Station, December, 1943.

———. *Religious Organization in Kentucky.* Lexington, Ky.: University of Kentucky, Agricultural Experiment Station, August, 1948. Bulletin 524.

Kumlien, W. F. *Community School Districts in the Making.* Brookings, South Dakota: South Dakota State College, Agricultural Experiment Station, June, 1950. Bulletin 404.

Landis, Benson Y. *Bethlehem and Rochdale.* Co-operative League of the U. S. A., 167 W. 12th St., New York 11, N. Y., 1944.

Lord, Russell. *To Hold This Soil.* Washington: United States Department of Agriculture, August, 1938. Miscellaneous Publication No. 321.

Mangus, A. R. *Mental Health of Rural Children in Ohio.* Wooster, Ohio: Ohio Agricultural Experiment Station, March, 1949. Bulletin 682.

Mather, William G., Jr. *The Rural Churches of Allegany County.* Ithaca, N. Y.: Cornell University Agricultural Experiment Station, March, 1934. Bulletin 587.

National Education Association. *A Policy for Rural Education in the United States.* Washington: National Education Association, 1940.

The People, the Land, and the Church in the Rural South. Mimeographed. Farm Foundation, 600 S. Michigan Ave., Chicago, Ill., 1941.

The People, the Land, and the Church in the Rural West. Mimeographed. Farm Foundation, 1943.

Raper, Arthur F. *The Japanese Village in Transition.* Tokyo: General Headquarters, Supreme Commander for the Allied Powers, 1950.

———. *A Graphic Presentation of Rural Trends.* Washington: Extension Service and Bureau of Agricultural Economics, United States Department of Agriculture, 1952.

Report of the Inquiry on Co-operative Enterprise in Europe, 1937. Washington: Government Printing Office, 1937.

Rich, Mark. *The Larger Parish, An Effective Organization for Rural Churches.* Ithaca, N. Y.: New York State College of Agriculture, Cornell University, May, 1939. Extension Bulletin 408.

Scheifele, Theodore C., and Mather, William G. *Closed Rural Pennsylvania Churches.* State College, Pennsylvania: Pennsylvania State College School of Agriculture, Agricultural Experiment Station, May, 1949. Bulletin 512.

A Self-Evaluation Scale for Town and Country Churches. Town and Country Department, Congregational Christian Church, 287 Fourth Avenue, New York 10, N. Y.

Sewell, William H. *The Construction and Standardization of a Scale for the Measurement of the Socio-economic Status of Oklahoma Farm Families.* Stillwater, Okla.: Oklahoma A. & M. College, Agricultural Experiment Station, April, 1940. Technical Bulletin 9.

215

Smith, Rose Marie. *Education in Rural and City School Systems.* Federal Security Agency.

Sumption, Merle R., and Beem, Harlan D. *A Guide to School Reorganization in Illinois.* University of Illinois Bulletin Number 59. University of Illinois, Urbana, Ill.

The White House Conference on Rural Education. National Education Association of the United States, 1201 Sixteenth Street, Northwest, Washington 6, D. C., 1945.

Whitman, Lauris B., and Mather, William G. *The Rural Churches of Four Pennsylvania Counties.* State College, Pennsylvania: School of Agriculture, Agricultural Experiment Station, June, 1952. Progress Report No. 76.

INDEX

217

254.2
Smbc
c.1.